101 Dumb Financial Mistakes
Business Owners Make
and How to Avoid Them

TESTIMONIALS

"I have made so many dumb financial mistakes in my businesses that I wish I had read Ruth King's book when I started my first company in 1990 so I could have been avoided most of them!"

—**Barry Moltz**, small business expert

"I have known Ruth King for over 20 years. We have shared the stage many times. Whenever she speaks, I always take notes. You've heard of a 'Dutch Uncle'? That is a man who tells you the truth that changes your life, even if you don't like what you hear. Ruth is a 'Dutch Auntie.' Her advice is always spot on, delivered with tough love. Her new book will change your business and life. Listen to her. She knows her stuff. Read this book. Follow her advice. Profit is not a dirty word…"

—**Mark Matteson**, international speaker and best-selling author of seven books

"Making mistakes in business is easy. Knowing how to fix them correctly and learn from them is the secret to success. Ruth helped me learn my mistake lessons. She can help you as well."

—**Mike Ratchford**, former business owner who sold his business for seven figures

"Sometimes business owners are lucky enough to find someone who makes a significant mark on the health and profitability of their business. Ruth King is that someone to the business owners she has served over the years. *101 Dumb Financial Mistakes Business Owners Make and How to Avoid Them* is a must-read book for any anyone who wants to learn how to avoid common financial mistakes, stay in business, and be profitable. King presents valuable information in an easily digestible way, offering the reader interesting, real-life examples to learn from so business owners avoid the same mistakes, stay in business, and remain profitable."

—**Heidi Salati**, director, education and training, PHCC National

"We called Ruth one night about five years ago thinking we were done. She helped us, and yes, we're still here. We made many of the mistakes that Ruth writes about. Save yourself a lot of sleepless nights and stress by learning from what she says."

—**Sonny Dukes**, founder and CEO, Accurate Power and Technology

"Ruth King is not an academic, thank God. She is a battle-scarred business owner and coach to many small business owners. Her latest book will show you where the profit-devouring quicksand is and how not to let it eat your business alive."

—**Jerry Bellune**, It's Your Business, the #2 small business authority

"Ruth King has done it again! Her latest book, *101 Dumb Financial Mistakes Business Owners Make and How to Avoid Them*, is nothing short of a masterpiece. No writer understands their audience better than King. She knows that business owners are busy and want to cut to the chase when it comes to getting their information. And that information is always practical and very accessible to the reader."

—**Kevin Price**, Host, Price of Business Radio, Nationally Syndicated and distributed by USA Business Radio. Publisher and Editor in Chief, USDailyReview.com

101 DUMB FINANCIAL
MISTAKES
BUSINESS OWNERS MAKE

... AND How to
Avoid Them

RUTH KING

NEW YORK

LONDON • NASHVILLE • MELBOURNE • VANCOUVER

101 DUMB FINANCIAL MISTAKES BUSINESS OWNERS MAKE AND HOW TO AVOID THEM

Published in New York, New York, by Morgan James Publishing. Morgan James is a trademark of Morgan James, LLC. www.MorganJamesPublishing.com

Proudly distributed by Ingram Publisher Services.

Morgan James BOGO™

A **FREE** ebook edition is available for you or a friend with the purchase of this print book.

CLEARLY SIGN YOUR NAME ABOVE

Instructions to claim your free ebook edition:
1. Visit MorganJamesBOGO.com
2. Sign your name CLEARLY in the space above
3. Complete the form and submit a photo of this entire page
4. You or your friend can download the ebook to your preferred device

ISBN 9781636980461 paperback
ISBN 9781636980478 ebook
Library of Congress Control Number: 2022945162

Cover Design by:
Rachel Lopez
www.r2cdesign.com

Interior Design by:
Chris Treccani
www.3dogcreative.net

Morgan James is a proud partner of Habitat for Humanity Peninsula and Greater Williamsburg. Partners in building since 2006.

Get involved today! Visit MorganJamesPublishing.com/giving-back

This book is dedicated to business owners in all types of businesses. May this book help you get and stay profitable, build wealth, and give back.

TABLE OF CONTENTS

FIGURES AND TABLES

READ THIS FIRST

Two men, Peter and Paul (not their real names), decide to start a business together. Peter and Paul had a great partnership. Each year the business increased their total revenues. After 12 years the business reached $2 million in revenue.

Peter and Paul never paid attention to the financial side of their company. They felt that as long as they had cash in the bank to pay their bills, cover payroll, and take their discounts, they were happy.

They never paid attention to profits or looked at the tax returns that the accountant compiled from their financial statements. When the accountant asked them for their inventory value, they guessed. They didn't have a clue what it really was.

The only thing that mattered to Peter and Paul was that they had enough cash to operate and do the things they needed and wanted to do.

When the company hit $2 million in revenue, growth stopped. Soon problems began to appear. Occasionally they couldn't take their discounts. They didn't always have the cash to make payroll.

They knew something was wrong. After all, they grew the company to $2 million in revenue without problems. Why now, at $2 million, were they having cash flow issues?

They were smart enough to get help. I analyzed their financial operations and determined that they had been losing a nickel for every dollar they took in the door for 12 years!

Because it was "just a nickel," the cash flow from revenues masked the problem since cash increased as the company grew. Since they never paid attention to profits and profitability, they never knew the company was unprofitable. The cash received from one project funded the next. As long as the number of projects kept increasing, the increasing cash flow kept the company alive.

When growth stopped, the lack of profits was exposed: lack of proper cash flow due to prices being too low…at least a nickel too low.

What happened? They raised their prices 10%, started earning a profit, and generated positive cash flow. The company didn't lose customers. In fact, many wondered how they could provide the quality of work they did as inexpensively as they did!

Growth hides profitability problems.

This story illustrates just one of the financial mistakes that business owners often make. By revealing these mistakes in this book, you will avoid them or stop doing them. This saves yourself heartaches and sleepless nights.

FOREWORD

I first met Ruth King when she was presenting a seminar in St. Louis, Missouri. I was a small contractor, working out of my man-cave garage, and wanted more. I hired her. She was expensive, but I took the plunge. Looking back, I would never have achieved the things I've wanted without her help. Ruth has more than paid back any investment I've made in her consulting services.

The first "argument" (OK, debate) we had was that I had to move out of my man-cave garage and spend $500 a month on rent. Ruth showed me how that payment would pay for itself in additional productivity and how we could generate the revenues to support it.

I did it. It more than paid for itself, and we quickly outgrew that space. The business was growing profitably and rapidly.

The next move was to an even bigger facility, and finally we have bought land to build our building so that we won't (I hope) have to move anymore. Ruth has guided us every step of the way.

Ruth taught me to run my business on net profit per hour basis and to share the profits with my employees and charities. The employees have seen good and bad years, meaning large and small bonuses. As long as the company makes a positive net profit per hour, we share the profit—even if the checks are really small. Employees always ask how the company is doing so they know what their share is likely to be. They want a positive bottom line and to perform profitably.

Then COVID-19 hit. I remember calling Ruth and thanking her for making me put 1% of all of the revenues received in a savings account along with all of the maintenance money (recurring revenue) received. I told Ruth that it didn't matter what happened. We had enough cash in the bank to survive.

Please read what Ruth writes in this book. Implement her suggestions. Don't make the mistakes she reveals. Ruth knows what she is talking about. She has helped me, and others, grow profitable businesses, build wealth, and achieve our goals.

Tim Schellert
CEO, Elite Mechanical, Inc.
Wentzville, Missouri

INTRODUCTION

The first time most business owners pay attention to the financial side of their company is when they get in trouble. They can't meet payroll, supplier bills are late, a huge customer who represents more than 20% of their business' revenues or worse profits leaves, or any other seemingly catastrophic situation occurs.

This potential catastrophe caused them to pay attention and delve into their financials. They become the second or, even better, the third type of business owner, according to my grandfather.

My grandfather always said that the first type of business owner makes mistakes and never learns from them. So, they make them over and over again. They waste a lot of time and money, and have a lot of heartaches and sleepless nights.

The second type makes mistakes too. However, they learn from them. The first time it hurts so bad that they never make that mistake again. Of course, they can still experience wasted time and money, and have a lot of heartaches and sleepless nights. But at least those sleepless nights are because of the first time they made that mistake.

The third type learns from the mistakes of others. They don't make those mistakes. Of course, they can make others that they haven't learned about. However, once they make those mistakes they learn from them, like the second type of business owner. They don't make them again.

Over the past 40+ years I've seen business owners and managers do some really dumb things. This book was written in hopes that you won't make those same mistakes. You'll be like the third type of business owner. You will probably make mistakes that I didn't write about in this book. However, you'll learn from them and never make those mistakes again.

There are three major types of businesses: lifestyle businesses, businesses used as a tool (I'll call them *tool businesses* for short), and transformational businesses. I describe each in the next section.

It is OK to be any type of business. It doesn't matter whether you are a lifestyle business—you're in business. You don't have to grow—except at the rate of inflation, so your bottom line profit stays consistent.

No business type is good or bad. It's totally up to you and your goals in life. Depending on your type of business, some of the mistakes in this book won't apply to you. I highlight the types of businesses where these mistakes can cause problems. Pay attention!

The Three Types of Businesses and How to Thrive in Each Type

"How do you know all business owners want to be profitable?"

This was a question posed to me by my mentor, Peter Diamandis.

I didn't have an answer. I was stunned into silence (and those of you who know me well know that I usually have an answer for almost every question).

Peter's question set me off on a very different path from the one I had been on—my premise before he asked that question was that I wanted to give the tools and processes to all businesses, worldwide, to help them get and stay profitable, build wealth, and give back. This book reveals the financial mistakes that business owners make and is part of my mission in life.

Now, the question: "What if a business owner didn't care about being profitable?" And yes, some of you don't care about being profitable even though profitability is critical for survival in any type of business.

I realized that there were really three types of businesses—lifestyle businesses, tool businesses, and transformation businesses (Table 1).

There is no one "right" type of business. Each type has a different focus. Each was started or purchased for a different reason. Each has a different result the owner desires.

This section describes each type of business and what they typically focus on.

TABLE 1. SUMMARY OF BUSINESS TYPES

Business type	Lifestyle	Tool	Transformation
Funding	None needed	Personal or family	Venture capital

Revenue growth	No growth	5–10% a year	10⊡ a year
Employees	1–2	2–100	100+
Cash	Critically important	Important	Critically important
Profit and loss statement	Not important	Very important	Critically important
Balance sheet	Ignored	Very important	Critically important
Recurring revenue	Critically important	Important	Important
Exit plan	None	Sell the business	Sell or go public

Lifestyle Businesses

Lifestyle businesses are started and operate to support the desired lifestyle of the business owner. Many times, it is a married couple.

Lifestyle business owners don't want employees. Their business is totally dependent on them to generate revenues.

These businesses don't need funding to start. The cash flow and revenues are dependent on the owner.

The owner cares about having enough cash coming in the door to live the lifestyle they desire. Multimillion-dollar lifestyle businesses exist.

The business owner might live on a beach, in the mountains, travel constantly, and do whatever pleases them. As long as there is enough cash, the owner is happy.

They might have a four-hour work week, as popularized by Tim Ferriss in his book *The 4-Hour Workweek.*

They might work a few weeks to generate enough revenue and then forget about business until cash needs come up again.

Rarely are their employees in lifestyle businesses. There might be a virtual assistant handing the billing and other operational issues, leaving the owner to do what they like to do.

As many business activities as possible are outsourced.

A lot has been written about lifestyle businesses not being real businesses. They are. They generate revenue and have profit, even if they don't pay attention to it. They monitor cash and make sure there is enough to support how they live.

Lifestyle business owners focus on and monitor three things:

1. Pricing for positive cash flow.
2. Having enough cash.
3. Having easy recurring revenue coming in the door at all times.

Tool Businesses

Tool businesses were started or bought for a personal purpose: to build so that they can pass it on to the next generation or to have the freedom to do specific things as the business grows, and perhaps eventually sell. These businesses are generally started with personal funds or loans from friends and family. As the business grows profitable, bank lines of credit or funding for asset purchases becomes possible.

For example, one business owner started his business so he had the freedom to attend all of his daughter's volleyball games (she was ranked nationally). The business was a tool to accomplish this goal.

This required building a profitable business and hiring employees to handle the day-to-day activities of the business while he was gone. Now that she is out of college, he is planning to sell the profitable business that he built.

Tool business owners focus on and monitor:

1. Employee satisfaction and productivity.
2. Financial statements (cash, profit and loss statement, balance sheet).
3. Recurring revenue to build the business.
4. Positive cash flow.

Transformation Businesses

Transformation businesses are started to impact millions or billions of people. They have exponential growth. Many are trying to solve world problems. The person or team starting or leading the business is a true entrepreneur.

Venture capital usually funds the business's exponential growth.

Transformation business owners think in terms of 10 times growth or more each year. A 10% growth rate is boring and reached in weeks or months.

Think about the exponential business owners and entrepreneurs you know of: Elon Musk, Jeff Bezos, Steve Jobs, Richard Branson. These entrepreneurs are changing the world.

Founders and managers of transformation businesses think differently than employees of other types of businesses. They are constantly searching for ways to exponentially grow the company. How can what they do be done faster, cheaper, better? Yes, sometimes they work themselves out of business.

The end of a transformation business is merging with another transformation business, a public offering, or sometimes bankruptcy. For example, some technology-based companies didn't keep up with changes and went out of business because they became obsolete.

Transformation business owners focus on and monitor:

- Employee creativity and risk taking. They have to fail!
- Financial statements (profit and loss statement, balance sheet).
- Positive cash flow.

All businesses, whether the business is a lifestyle, tool, or transformation business, must avoid the mistakes revealed in the next sections to survive and thrive.

|||||||||||||||||||||||||||||||||||||||||||

Dumb Mistakes:

General

|||||||||||||||||||||||||||||||||||||||||||

These are common mistakes that are not related
to your pricing, profit and loss statement,
balance sheets or theft.

1

Believing That Profit Is a Bad Word

||||||||||||||||||||||||||||||||||||||||||

Some business owners are ashamed to make a profit. They think profit is bad. As a result they don't price profitably, and then they struggle. They work themselves harder than they would if they were employees of another company. The lack of profit causes cash flow problems, and they experience sleepless nights and stress.

Profit is necessary for business survival. Even lifestyle businesses, which focus more on cash than profits, need profitable revenues. Those profits are turned into cash to support the owners' lifestyle.

For transformation businesses that are exponentially growing, profit is not as important as cash as growth expands. When Jeff Bezos was starting Amazon, he stated that he didn't care if the company ever made a profit. What he did watch was net cash per hour (rather than net profit per hour). He had to make sure he had the cash to grow. Profits came later. Pricing must eventually incorporate profitable revenues, or the company can implode if it stops growing.

What is profit used for? First, it must be turned into cash. Cash is necessary to fund payroll and other business expenses. Profit is used to fund growth, increasing salaries, increasing inventory (if you have inventory), and increasing overhead expenses. Without sufficient cash, businesses will die.

How much profit is too much? That answer is totally up to you. It depends on your growth goals, your giving goals, and what you want out of your business.

Profit is good. Profit is necessary for business survival. You decide how much profit you want to earn.

2

Abdicating the Responsibility for the Financial Side of Your Company

IIIIIIIIIIIIIIIIII|IIIIIIIIIIIIIIIII

"I hired a bookkeeper. Now I don't have to worry about the books anymore."

The first office person an owner hires is usually a bookkeeper. Then they ignore the financial side of the company because they think, *It's being taken care of.*

Theft often happens when you stop paying attention to the financial part of your company. You can delegate responsibility for day-to-day bookkeeping activities. You cannot abdicate the responsibility for the financial side of your company. You must retain oversight and review every week and every month. It's your business. You have to oversee all of it, including financials.

Your financial statements are your scorecard. You have to know what they are telling you so you can spot minor issues and take care of them before they become major crises.

By the 15th of each month, your bookkeeper should give you a profit and loss (P&L) statement and a balance sheet. Your P&L is also called an income statement.

They should also give you supporting documents, an aged receivables report, an aged payables report, and reconciliation reports.

The earlier you receive these reports, the sooner you can review them and take care of minor issues before they become major crises. In the old days, we had to wait until our bank statements came through snail mail, so the 15th of the month was the norm. Now you can see your bank statements every day on line. No more excuses!

First, review your financial statements. In less than a minute you can spot these 10 mistakes (detailed explanations are given later in this book).

1. Are you using accrual accounting? (see Mistake 7)

This means you see accounts receivable, accounts payable, and inventory (if you have inventory) on your balance sheet. QuickBooks tells you whether the statement is printed on a cash or an accrual basis in the upper left-hand corner. If you are not using QuickBooks or if you don't see accounts receivable, accounts payable, or inventory on your balance sheet, your financial statements are probably not accurate from an operations basis (they may be from a tax basis—but the IRS doesn't run your business on a day-to-day basis). Accrual accounting is critical for good financial analysis and for spotting minor issues before they become major crises.

2. Does your balance sheet balance?

Assets should balance with liabilities plus net worth (or equity). If it doesn't, then someone is not putting entries into your accounting system properly or QuickBooks needs to be rebalanced (you usually get a notice that it is not in balance).

3. Do you have negative cash on your balance sheet? (see Mistake 5)

You can't have negative cash in your checking account. The bank would charge you large fees and close your account. More than likely you have a lazy bookkeeper who prints out all the checks at once and sends them out when there is money to pay the bills. Don't print checks unless you have money in the bank to cover them.

4. Is your inventory (if you have it) the same number every month, or is it not on the balance sheet? (see Mistake 56)

The likelihood that inventory is the same value each month is about the likelihood of winning the lottery. Inventory changes every day depending on the materials ordered and the materials used to produce products and services.

5. Do you have negative payroll taxes on your balance sheet? (see Mistake 65)

The IRS probably doesn't owe you money. Your state revenue department probably doesn't owe you money. This is a bookkeeping error. Get the accounting for your payroll expenses correct. It affects your entire financial statement.

6. Do you have negative loan balances on your balance sheet? (see Mistake 64)

The bank doesn't owe you money for your loan payments. Again, this is a bookkeeping error. This usually happens when the entire loan payment is deducted from the loan balance. Part of the payment is principal and part is interest expense. Make sure the interest expense shows up on your P&L and the principal reduction is shown on your balance sheet.

7. Do you have a negative gross profit on your profit and loss statement? (see Mistake 81)

Gross profit is sales minus cost of goods sold. Unless you knowingly have a loss leader (like some supermarket sales that lure you into the store by, for example, selling a gallon of milk for $1), you don't purchase a part for $10 and sell it for $8.

The only time this might happen—and it is rare—is when all you do in a month is warranty work. Then you have almost no revenue and large costs for providing the warranty to your customers.

8. Do you have no rent, utility, or other normal monthly expenses? (see Mistake 88)

Make sure these bills are recorded each month. You have to pay your rent every month or your landlord will kick you out of your office.

9. Is your net profit on your profit and loss statement the same as your current retained earnings on your balance sheet?

If not, then you have a problem. The net profit on your P&L should be exactly the same as the current retained earnings on your balance sheet. If it isn't, then someone is probably making journal entries that should not be made.

10. Do your aged accounts receivable and aged accounts payable balance reports match the values shown on your balance sheet? (see Mistakes 61 and 63)

They should match exactly. If they don't, then someone is putting journal entries into the system to cause the imbalance. Find out why.

3

Having Mercedes-Benz Syndrome

|||||||||||||||||||||||||||||||||||||||||

A colleague was helping a business owner look for funding for his business. He introduced him to a potential investor at lunch. The next day the investor called my colleague and told him that the person was nice but he would never invest in his business. My colleague asked why. The investor said that he had "Mercedes-Benz syndrome".

"What's that?" asked my colleague. The investor explained that during the conversation at lunch, he found out that this person was funding a $2,200 Porsche lease through the business. He appeared interested in having the business pay for his personal lifestyle. The investor explained to my colleague that his money was not going to pay for a car lease. His investments were supposed to help grow the business, not the owner's personal "finer things in life." He went on to explain that he called this the "Mercedes-Benz syndrome," where the business pays for unnecessary personal assets, such as the owner's Mercedes-Benz. Investment that is supposed to go toward the business's needs goes toward the owner's personal needs.

It struck me that a lot of company owners do this too. These are the owners who don't understand that cash does not mean profits and that having cash does not mean that you have to spend it. These are the owners who use business cash to buy boats, have the company pay for expensive trucks and cars, write off vacations, build expensive homes, have nonworking relatives on the payroll, and so on. Instead of investing in the business, they invest in themselves.

Don't get me wrong. There is absolutely nothing wrong with enjoying the fruits of your labor. However, you can't do it at the expense of your business. You have to save cash for the downturns. You have to save for a rainy day.

So how do you avoid Mercedes-Benz syndrome? You make sure that you are earning enough on products to generate reasonable profits. You save some of the money you generate from collections on those sales (see Mistake 73).

Hopefully you don't have Mercedes-Benz syndrome. Good profits and savings will prevent you from a financial hardship in years to come.

4

Blindly Accepting What
Your CPA Reports on Your Taxes

||||||||||||||||||||||||||||||||||||||

This mistake could cause a business owner to pay taxes on $90,000 in phantom income. Here's what happened.

A business owner changes accounting software and accounting firms in 2012. There is an accounts receivable note from another company for $90,000 in the new QuickBooks software that was in the old accounting software when the change is made.

The new CPA reports this note on the company's Schedule L tax return in 2012 as an owner's note receivable rather than a note receivable from another company.

The new CPA blindly made this assumption rather than getting the details about this note. This is where the problem started.

The owner doesn't question the 2012 tax return and simply signs it as correct.

This receivable is still on the books 10 years later. No payments were made from the other company in the past 10 years.

It has simply been reported for 10 years as an owner's receivable rather than a note receivable from the other company.

Every year, for 10 years, the owner sees the balance sheet and the accounts receivable owner's note on it. It's the same number every year. The owner never questions it. He doesn't think anything about it.

Every year the CPA reports the owner's note receivable on the Schedule L tax return.

It's been wrong for 10 years. No one said anything or did anything about it until I started questioning the financial statements.

You, as an owner, can't make good business decisions on inaccurate financial statements. Garbage in equals garbage out.

So, how do you correct the balance sheet? How do you get this owner's note receivable off the books because the owner doesn't owe the money?

You can't just write it off. It has been on the tax return for 10 years. You don't want to refile amended tax returns. It is expensive and will probably trigger a red flag and a potential IRS audit.

In addition, if there were an audit, the owner signed 10 years of tax returns with this owner's note receivable on it. His signature says the taxes are correct—including this owner's note receivable. Imagine explaining that you didn't see it for 10 years in an IRS audit.

The only legal way to get the receivable off the balance sheet is for the owner to write a check to the company for the $90,000. Then the owner's receivable is satisfied.

If the owner wants his $90,000 back (could be as a distribution or salary), he will have to pay taxes on the $90,000.

You might say, "just leave the owner note on the balance sheet." You could. However, if you were to sell the company, pass it to the next generation, or close the company, this owner's note receivable will affect your selling price or final tax return.

Always review what your CPA reports on your tax returns before you sign and submit them. Make sure they are correct. If you don't understand something or think something is not correct, ask! It could save you thousands of dollars.

5

Having Only One Bank

||||||||||||||||||||||||||||||||||||

When I wrote the *Ugly Truth about Small Business* in 2003, this story got my attention. Since that time I have always cultivated relationships with more than one bank.

The story is summarized here so you can learn from this business owner's mistake.

My banker caused my entrepreneurial terror. To understand why, you need to know my background. I've always been a grave dancer. I couldn't afford anything when I started in business. I had to buy something that had problems, either a business or a building that needed turning around so I could afford it. I always had to modify it and do a lot to make it successful. I had some good fortune doing this and some good experiences. I had built profitable, successful businesses over the years using the bank's money. My banker almost put that to an end in an afternoon.

I had to go into business for myself. I loved foreign cars. It was a time period when everyone thought foreign cars might become 2 or 3% of the total cars in the US. I was convinced that they were going to be 20%, so I opened up a gas station in Oshkosh, Wisconsin, that specialized in repairing foreign cars. It expanded into a body shop, which expanded to a parts store and then on into Green Bay.

Not totally satisfied with owning only a gas station, body shop, and more, I was buying distressed duplexes and fixing them up. Then I began to convert duplexes to commercial properties. Then I acquired more businesses.

All of the businesses' accounts, loans, and real estate, including my own home, were with one bank that I had a great relationship with. A new president took over and almost killed everything.

Back in those days, generally you established a relationship with a local bank. They look at you, and they look at your financials and your accomplishments, and I had accomplished a lot by then. Everything was running smoothly, and I was current on everything with nothing bouncing or past due accounts. I owed the bank about $3 million.

One day I got a call from my loan officer. He said that the president of the bank wants to talk with me. I had to be here at 1 p.m. the next afternoon and bring my business partner. It was a little odd that the president wasn't coming to see me, but I didn't think anything of it.

When I got to the bank, the loan officer and I walked into the president's office. These were his exact words. "I want you to get all your f---ing accounts out this bank today."

Terror hit. I said, "What are you talking about?"

He said, "I don't want your f---ing loans in here, I don't want your personal stuff in here, and you have some sort of stupid loan in here that is almost $250,000 that we pay the interest and that's not legal."

I said, "That's not correct."

He countered, "Yes it is, and I don't want to hear anything more about it".

The bank president was screaming. Everyone in the office could hear him. Everyone could hear his bad language. I was in shock. He wanted my checking account and everything out that day. He said that if I didn't do it today, he would start actions against every one of my items. I told him that I had payroll to make that Friday (the meeting was on a Tuesday). He said he really didn't care. He told me I was not using the line of credit to do it. The avalanche was about ready to begin.

I walked out of there reeling. My partner was in tears. I was very angry. I went back to work thinking, *Oh boy, all these years of work, and this whole thing is going to roll on back down. It's going to be a matter of selling assets and seeing if I can keep everything together.* I just stayed at work and thought about it.

I finally went home. It was the only time, in all of those years, my wife had ever seen me worried and stressed out about what I was going to do. I just didn't see any way out. My world was crashing in because of an irrational bank president who didn't know what he was doing when it came to loans.

Once the emotion stopped, I started thinking rationally. I just took one thing at a time. My attorney reviewed the loan documents and proved that the bank had to give us 30 days' notice when calling the loans. On Friday I called my loan officer and told him I wanted to talk to the president of the bank. He said no, I couldn't do that. So, I said, "He needs to talk to my attorney then. The bank will honor my line of credit to pay payroll because of the agreement the bank signed with me. I will be running a payroll and those checks will clear."

I got a message from the president by phone saying the bank will honor the line of credit until the end of the month. It took me less than 30 days to solve each of the banking issues. I did it one thing at a time.

Always have a relationship with more than one bank. You never know when a bank will get sold or new management will take over and change the loan policies. If this happens and your bank calls a loan, giving you 30 days to repay it, you have other options with other bankers you've built a relationship with.

6

Not Copying Checks and Deposits before Making the Deposit

||||||||||||||||||||||||||||||||||||||||

"We are debiting your bank account for $8,235."

This was the notice that a business owner received in the mail.

The bookkeeper knew that she hadn't made a mistake in the deposit. She reviewed the deposit and realized that $8,235 was the exact amount of one of the checks that she had deposited.

She went to the bank with copies of the deposit slip, the checks, and the adding machine tape showing the deposit was correct.

The bank had lost a check!

If she hadn't made copies of the checks before she deposited them, the company would have lost $8,235 in revenues.

Making copies of all checks prior to depositing them in the bank ensures that your bookkeeper's addition is correct and the deposit is correct.

If your company has remote deposit (you can deposit checks from your company location), it's important to keep all the checks you deposit remotely as long as your bank requires you to keep them.

Banks do make mistakes on occasion. Make sure you keep records of what you deposit.

7

Being on a Cash Basis for Accounting

||||||||||||||||||||||||||||||||||

"Oh, crap. I knew we were losing money even though our profit and loss statement said we were profitable."

This is what a business owner said when she switched her books from cash-based reporting to accrual reporting.

How could this be? In cash basis accounting, the only time an expense is recorded is when the bill is paid. The only time a sale is recorded is when you get the money for that sale (sales are revenue in cash accounting—see Mistake 75). There are no accounts receivable or accounts payable in cash-based accounting.

In accrual accounting, revenues are recorded when the bill is sent to the customer, whether or not the customer has paid the bill. An expense is recorded when the invoice is received, whether or not it has been paid. There are accounts receivable and accounts payable in accrual accounting.

In this case the company was almost always profitable because they didn't pay their bills unless they had the cash to pay them! In the months when there was a lot of cash to pay bills that had accumulated, the company could show a loss (more expenses than receipts).

In accrual accounting, an expense is recorded even if the bill isn't paid. The owner saw that when the revenues and expenses were recorded at the time they were incurred, she could easily make sure that all expenses for the projects were deducted from the revenues for that project. She discovered that the company performed work that wasn't profitable!

The company's accountant told her that for her company, it was better to report taxes on a cash basis. However, she could operate her business on an accrual basis. It was up to her.

Operate your company's accounting on an accrual basis. Your financial statements show your accounts payable, accounts receivable, and inventory levels. You'll know each month, assuming your data is accurate, whether your company is really profitable.

8

Ignoring Your Weekly Cash Flow Report

|||||||||||||||||||||||||||||||||||||||

"Sometimes you have to be hit between the eyes with a 2 × 4."

Here is what happened because an owner was too busy to pay attention to cash.

The company's bookkeeper sends me the company's weekly cash flow report, aged receivables report, aged payables report, and weekly sales budget every Friday. She also sends it to the owner and managers.

The weekly cash flow report (Figure 1) states the amount of cash at the beginning of the week, what was collected, and what was disbursed. She then estimates cash in and cash out for the following week based on payables and receivables.

The weekly sales budget is a revenue budget based on the overall budget for the year. It breaks down the monthly sales goals into weekly goals for all of the departments. It's an easy way to make sure the company is on track from a revenue perspective.

Until September the company was making its revenue budget almost every week, and for the weeks they didn't make budget, the revenues the following week or weeks more than made up for the deficit.

They missed the revenue budget the first week in September. It was Labor Day week and potentially a little slower. Nothing to worry about or take action on.

The company missed the revenue budget the next week. Now it was time to be a little concerned. I sent back an email asking whether everything was billed, if work was slowing down, etc. If it was slowing down, we could have done some marketing to generate revenue. I was told that there were some large jobs coming up and that we would see them in upcoming weeks.

This email sequence got louder and louder because the company barely made budget through December. I watched the ending cash go down each week. I got no response to my inquiries and concerns.

The week of Christmas, I got an email from the owner saying they were out of money and asking how this happened!

I asked him whether he even looked at the weekly reports and my emails about them. He said not often.

Sometimes you have to be hit between the eyes with a 2 × 4 to pay attention!

Review your weekly cash flow report every week. Your bookkeeper should put it on your desk before they leave on Friday afternoon along with a list of aged payables and aged receivables. Review the reports. Circle the bills you want paid so your bookkeeper can prepare the checks for your signature. Look at the aged receivables and circle any customers you want to have called about collection and follow up.

This is the best way to make sure you have enough money for payroll the following week and to make sure you know which customers owe your company money and which vendors must be paid.

WEEKLY CASH REPORT

Week of _____ Prepared by _____

Cash on hand at the beginning of the week:

Petty cash	$ _____
Checking account 1	$ _____
Checking account 2	$ _____
Payroll account	$ _____
Money market	$ _____
Other savings	$ _____
Total beginning cash	$ _____
Cash collected	$ _____
Credit card payments collected	$ _____
Accounts receivable collected	$ _____
Other inputs (loans etc.)	$ _____
TOTAL AVAILABLE CASH FOR THE WEEK	$ _____

Disbursements:

Payroll	$ _____
Accounts payable	$ _____
Loan payment	$ _____
Other	$ _____
Total disbursements	$ _____
ENDING CASH FOR WEEK	$ _____

Estimated requirements for next week:

Accounts receivable to be collected	$ _____
Payroll	$ _____
Accounts payable to be paid	$ _____
Loan payments due	$ _____
TOTAL ESTIMATED CASH SURPLUS (NEEDS) NEXT WEEK	$ _____

9

Not Understanding the Difference between Cash, Profits, and Profitability

||||||||||||||||||||||||||||||||||||||||||||

Which is more important cash, cash flow, or profits?

Operating your business on a cash basis is not smart. Operating your business on profits is OK. Operating your business on profitability is best.

When you operate your business on cash you have no clue if you are profitable or not. You only know if you have cash in the bank to pay your bills. As long as you are growing, even if you are not profitable, you will have the cash. (See the "Read This First" story at the beginning of this book).

What's wrong with operating your business on profit? Actually, nothing.

But operating on profit is a short-term view. If you have profit one month, you may or may not have a profit the second month. And you don't know whether your profits are increasing on a long-term basis since you are focused solely on the month-to-month profit. You might get really concerned with a loss one month and forget about the following month because the company was profitable. Yo-yo profit and loss can be a recipe for disaster.

The best way to operate your business? Profitability.

Profitability is sustained profits. It is the ability to always fund operations through the profits of your company. A month's loss is concerning, and the reasons for the loss need to be determined. However, if the company has increasing profitability, the one-month loss will not kill the company.

Focus on profitability, then profits, and then as long as you collect your money, you will have enough cash to run operations.

Positive cash flow is more important than cash.

Cash is critical so that you can pay for rent, utilities, and other business expenses. But how do you get cash? Through cash flow!

Imagine a tank of water. And, instead of water in the tank, there is cash in the tank.

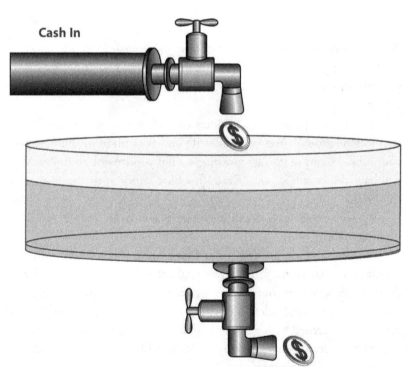

Figure 2. Cash flow tank

If you never added to it, then the tank would drain as you paid for your rent, payroll, supplies, utilities, and more. At some point there would not be any cash left in the tank, and you would be out of business.

Cash flow is necessary to get cash. You have to have cash coming in so that you can pay for what you want and need. Payments are cash out.

How do you get cash inputs? The majority of the time through collections on sales. Notice I didn't say *sales*. If you send out an invoice for work you performed, you have an account receivable, not cash. You cannot use an account receivable to pay the rent!

When the customer pays, that is a collection and you can add that cash to the tank. When you have an account receivable, you are the bank for the customer. Retailers, restaurants, and many other businesses have decided that they don't want to be banks. They get their money immediately upon services rendered. (Health care companies get their deductible immediately and some even request full payment. You are responsible for getting it back from the insurance company.)

Other cash inputs are from borrowing on lines of credit or personal savings, interest on investments, or, infrequently, a sale of an asset.

Cash outflows are payments you make for payroll, accounts payable, loan repayments, and occasionally taxes and asset purchases.

Open the spigot at the top and cash comes in. The level of cash rises. Open the drain and cash goes out. The level of cash falls. At the end of the month there has to be at least a penny in the tank to stay in business.

Beware of the slowly leaking tank! This is what happened to Peter and Paul in the story at the beginning of this book. This is where you get cash inputs so that you can pay your bills. At the end of the month you have a little less cash in the tank than you should have because of unprofitable jobs. The next month has the same scenario. At the end of this month, even with cash inputs, there is less water at the end of the month than there should be.

Don't be lulled into a false sense of security with cash inputs. You have to have more inputs than outgoes so that the level of cash in the tank remains constant or gets higher—that is, you have to have profits to turn into positive cash flow.

Cash is critical. Without positive cash flow, you will eventually have no cash.

10

Running Out of Money Because You Grew Too Fast

IIIIIIIIIIIIIIIII|IIIIIIIIIIIIIIIII

Lifestyle businesses don't run out of cash because of growth.

Tool businesses can grow out of business.

Transformation businesses have to pay attention to their cash flow because they always grow exponentially. If transformation businesses are unprofitable, they have to continue growing until they become profitable (see below).

Here's the rule of thumb to know when tool businesses are growing too fast and the rule of thumb to estimate how much cash is needed to grow.

First, some definitions:

- **Working capital:** Current assets minus current liabilities.
- **Current assets:** Cash or assets that are turned into cash within a year. Generally, current assets are cash, accounts receivable, inventory, and prepaid expenses. Those of you who are commercial may have work in progress as a current asset too. Make sure current assets are accurate (see Mistake 58).
- **Current liabilities:** Accounts payable and other debts that must be paid within a year. Generally, current liabilities are accounts payable, taxes payable, deferred income for recurring revenue enrollments, and current portion of long-term debt. Make sure current liabilities are accurate (see Mistake 58).
- **Annualized sales:** What you estimate your annual sales to be at any month for your fiscal year. Of course, year-end numbers are best. However, how do you annualize sales if it is May and your year-end is December? Annualized sales equal the total

of January through May sales times 12 divided by 5 (the fifth month of your fiscal year).

How to Determine If Your Company Is Growing Too Fast

Annualized sales divided by working capital is 10 or higher. It should be over 10 for transformation businesses. It should *not* be over 10 for tool businesses or lifestyle businesses.

If the result is under 10 for lifestyle and tool businesses, then the company probably is not growing too fast.

Here Is the Rule of Thumb for Cash Needs As a Company Grows

Ten percent of the anticipated growth in cash to survive the growth. For example, if the company's plan is to grow from $1,000,000 to $2,000,000 in sales, you need $100,000 in cash to fund that growth.

Do your cash planning to make sure you don't run out of cash as the company grows.

11

Not Billing

||||||||||||||||||||||||||||||||||

I walked into a client's office, and there was a stack of papers on his desk.

"What's that?" I asked.

"That's the customers whose work we have done that I haven't billed for yet."

"You're kidding."

"Nope. We've been too busy to bill."

That stack had two months of completed work that the customers had not been billed for.

You are *never* too busy to bill for the work you completed!

Imagine the surprise the customers got when they finally received a bill for the work that was completed two months ago. They've probably forgotten about it. They don't remember how much time it took or what they agreed to.

Even worse, this thought probably went through their head: *If that company took two months to send me a bill, I'm going to take two months to pay them. They probably don't need the money.*

The worst possible scenario: the money they had to pay that bill two months ago was spent on other things, so they don't have the money to pay it now.

Billing every day or as often as possible is critical for cash flow. Without billing, you won't get the cash that is owed to you quickly so you can use it to pay your bills.

Just as important, make sure that your billing is correct. When starting a long project, your accounts receivable person should call the accounts payable department at the company you are doing the work for, introduce themself, and explain that your company is starting a new project with that company. Ask what the billing requirements are to get paid on time. Discover whether you need specific purchase orders, signature sign-offs on the bill, documentation proving that the work was done, or other requirements. Then, when the bill is overdue and accounts receivable calls the company because you haven't received payment, they won't hear "this was missing from the invoice" and have to wait even longer to get paid.

When you send the first invoice, call that person again to make sure that everything is correct so that the payment is made on time.

Bill every day when possible. For longer projects, ask for a deposit to start the project, and bill at least once a month.

12

Focusing on the Top Line Rather Than the Bottom Line

|||||||||||||||||||||||||||||||||||||||

This was a conversation between an accountant and his client last year when they were reviewing the business owner's taxes:

"You had a great year."

"Not really."

"Why?"

"Look at my bottom line. It really didn't change from last year."

The CPA was focused on the top line growth. The business owner was focused on bottom line growth.

It's not how much you generate. It's how much you keep.

Volume is vanity. Profits are sanity.

The top line is important, but the bottom line is more important. Many small business owners brag about revenue growth, but almost no one brags about profit growth. Track overhead cost per hour (see Mistake 42) and net profit per hour (see Mistake 43) to ensure that your company is profitable as you grow. Calculate these two figures on a yearly basis, and review them every quarter.

Shift your focus from growing the top line to growing the bottom line—your net profit.

Reasons why revenues may have increased:

- The company raised prices because of increased material/equipment cost, then the company really was treading water.

- If the company's net profit per hour was exactly the same, even though the revenues were up, then the company really was treading water.
- If the company's net profit per hour was lower, even though the revenues were up, then the company is probably going backward (an explanation is needed here too).
- If the company's net profit per hour was higher, with higher revenues, then the company is probably going in the right direction.

Remember, net profit per hour is net operating profit divided by billable or revenue-producing hours. Looking at it another way: for each revenue-producing or billable hour, how much net operating profit drops to the bottom line?

Digging even deeper:

- If the average ticket price or average project revenue was increased just to cover the additional costs, then the company is treading water.
- If the average ticket price or average project revenue is higher because employees are adding additional services/products, then the company is doing better.
- If the closing ratio is higher than last year, then the company is doing better.

It's just as important to understand why revenues were higher and profits remained constant so that you can continue doing the things that are going well and take care of the things that are not going well.

The most important thing to track, in my opinion, is net profit per hour. If it is increasing, that is trending in the right direction. Discover why the company is doing better. If it is decreasing, find out why.

It's important to see an increasing revenue top line in your business. It's more important to see an increasing bottom line.

13

Refusing to Share the Wealth

||||||||||||||||||||||||||||||||||||

"He can afford it. He's made of money."

That's what employees think when they don't understand costs and profit. When you establish a bonus structure, employees learn about cost and profit. They care because it impacts their compensation.

Bonuses and profit sharing plans are put in place to reward managers and employees for helping the company achieve profits. Company owners share the wealth with those who have helped create it.

Bonuses and profit sharing are usually distributed two months after the fiscal year ends. They are distributed according to the program described below for managers and a separate program for all other employees. They are not distributed at holiday time, because if they are distributed at holiday time, then employees look at the distributions as gifts and expect them whether the company has a good year or a loss.

Bonuses are divided into two areas: manager bonuses and employee bonuses.

Manager Bonus Plan

The role of a good manager is to profitably take care of customers and employees. As such, all department managers participate in a program that rewards managers for the performance of their department. Bonuses are based on the following schedule.

Each manager's department is individually evaluated to determine profitability. If profits are realized, the department manager participates in sharing a percentage of those profits. The percentage of profits paid to each manager is equal to the percentage of profit their department achieved (before extraordinary expenses).

Net operating profit is defined as normal sales minus those expenses that the department normally experiences before bonuses and extraordinary expenses are deducted (for example, the owner deciding to take a bonus).

Example 1: Department Manager A runs a department that nets a 10% overall net operating profit on gross sales of $600,000. Department A had profits of $60,000. Department Manager A would then receive 10% of the profits for their department (in this case 10% of $60,000, or $6,000).

Example 2: The department has sales of $600,000 and nets 15%, or $90,000. Department Manager A would then receive 15% of the $90,000, or a $13,500.00 bonus.

The accounting department manager usually receives 1% of the profits of each department.

Inventory adjustments are factored in prior to managers' bonus calculations.

Managers' ability to manage their departments directly affects their bonus compensation. The better the profitability, the higher the bonus.

Employee Bonus Plan

Employees are paid based on their compensation (hourly wage plus bonus or salary) and the number of years of employment. The company owner determines the percentage of net operating profit to be distributed each year. Generally, this percentage ranges from 10% to 25%. The remainder is kept for company growth, manager bonuses, and owner distributions.

Employee bonuses are calculated according to each employee's percentage of the total compensation and number of years employed for all employees.

Example:

Employee 1: $20,000 total compensation; employed 3 years

Employee 2: $60,000 total compensation; employed 1 year

Employee 3: $30,000 total compensation, employed 5 years

To calculate Employee 1's bonus:

The company total number is: (20,000 ⊡ 3) + (60,000 ⊡ 1) + (30,000 ⊡ 5)

= 270,000

Employee 1 percentage is 60,000 / 270,000 = 22%

If the net operating profit to be distributed is $10,000, then Employee 1's bonus is $2,200.

14

Not Asking Employees to Participate in the Company Financial Goals

||||||||||||||||||||||||||||||||||

"You can't do it alone."

Ask for help from your employees. They usually have great ideas that could help the company. If managers don't ask, they'll never get suggestions that could really help when problems arise or ideas to help growth.

Here's an example. Year after year, February was a company's worst revenue month of the year. The owner was sick of this trend and decided to do something about it. He looked at the February monthly revenue for the past three years. Then he chose a minimum revenue goal that was a stretch but possible to attain.

The owner presented the idea to the entire company. He told them what the revenue numbers had been in the previous years. Then he asked them what they thought the company could do if everyone pitched in and came up with ideas that could be executed. (He didn't tell them his revenue goal.) The group came up with a higher revenue goal than he thought. It was a stretch, but no one thought it was impossible to achieve.

Assuming the company reached the goal, the owner would take everyone and their spouses or significant others out for a steak dinner at a great steak restaurant in town. And the company paid for babysitters so that everyone could go and enjoy an evening out. The company reached this goal.

Why? Everyone came up with ideas and leads. They were implemented, and great results occurred. The company met the goal and everyone had a fun evening out.

The contest doesn't have to be a company revenue contest. It could be a lead contest, an increase in billable hours (see Mistake 19), or something else to improve an area in your company.

It is critical to track and communicate the efforts and results. A thermometer or another type of chart posted on the wall is a great way to let everyone know progress toward the goal. It should be updated daily or at least weekly.

Choose a one-month goal or a three-month goal. Ask employees what reward they would like for reaching the goal. Make sure that all employees have input and believe that the goal can be met. Most business owners who have implemented this contest are shocked at who comes up with the greatest ideas and how motivated everyone can get.

The bottom line is that everyone wins—the customer, the employees, and the company.

15

Running Your Business by the Seat of Your Pants

IIIIIIIIIIIIIII|IIIIIIIIIIIIIIII

"You owe the IRS $25,000 in taxes."

"Why? Where is it?"

"You were very profitable this year."

If you don't know your numbers, you will probably get this type of call from your CPA at tax time too. Surprise! You had a really profitable year and owe taxes.

Budgeting and tracking the results prevents this type of surprise phone call from your CPA.

But how should the budget be created? Unfortunately, many times this budget is not based on actual planned revenues and costs: just add 5% to revenues or just add 7% to expenses. Doing this "throw a dart at a dartboard" budgeting does a business more harm than good.

Why? Because there isn't a plan for how revenues will be increased. There isn't a plan for increased expenditures like payroll raises, insurance, or other costs. Some expenses will increase more than 7%; others will remain the same.

Many owners decide what revenues they want to generate each year and then discover what the profit is at those revenue levels. If they don't like the profits, then they increase the revenues. So, they actually are determining the profits they want in their heads and then adjusting the revenues to meet the profits.

What if you first decided what profit you wanted, then determined the revenues that you needed to generate those profits? What if you started at the bottom of your profit and loss statement and worked up?

Once you know the revenue you need at the level of profit desired, determine how to generate it. This is bottom-up budgeting. Here's how you do it:

1. Write down your company's profit seasonality. You might lose money in January, February, and March. You might earn great profits in June, July, and August. These are the percentages that you earn each month. And yes, there can be negative months. However, what if you had zero profit those months rather than a negative profit those months?

2. Once you know the percentages each month, determine the total profit dollars you want to generate. Multiply each month's percentage by the total dollars. Then you know the total dollars you will earn each month.

3. Determine your monthly overhead. Look at your actual monthly overhead, add the amount of salary increases, insurance increases, and other additions, and you have your monthly overhead estimates.

4. Add the monthly net profit and overhead.

5. This gives you the monthly gross profit you must earn.

6. Look at your monthly gross margins (gross margin is gross profit divided by sales). These should be fairly consistent from month to month.

7. Divide your monthly budget gross profit by monthly gross margin. This is the revenue that you must generate each month.

Now, determine out how to generate that revenue!

Then, every month when you get your financial statements, compare the actual results to budgeted results. Where were you higher? Lower? And most important, why were you higher or lower? If your revenues were higher than expected, what can you do to continue this trend? If your expenses were higher than budgeted, what do you need to do to decrease the expenses in future months?

One more thing: don't put your budget in QuickBooks.

Most of you are probably thinking, *I shouldn't put a budget into QuickBooks? That's insane!*

Yes, budgeting from the bottom up is critical. But how most accounting software packages use budgets is a recipe for a false sense of security.

In most programs, when you enter a budget, it reports actual against budget for the month and potentially year to date.

That doesn't give you the data to make good business decisions.

Budgeting should be based on what you've generated and what you've spent year to date. This gives you the information to know whether you have spent too much, whether your revenues are lower or higher than budget, and much more.

Table 2 shows a budget and actual results.

At the beginning of the year, budget versus actual is all the same color. I show actuals for two months (the actual amounts are highlighted in gray). The company budgeted $2,200,000 for the year. After two months, assuming the company makes budget for the rest of the year, the actual revenues will be $2,214,437. Maintenance revenues are ahead of budget. Two months into the year, the company is just about on budget with respect to revenues. QuickBooks doesn't tell you this.

Total gross profit is budgeted to be $1,211,283, and year to date it is $1,219,824, assuming the company makes budget for the rest of the year. Again, after two months, the company is about $8,000 over budget.

You can see the actual expenses against the budgeted overhead expenses. You can see if you are spending too much or are on budget for the yearly amounts. QuickBooks doesn't tell you this information.

TABLE 2. BUDGET VERSUS ACTUAL RESULTS

	Jan 7%	Feb 7%	Mar 7%	Apr 7%	May 8%	Jun 9%	Jul 9%	Aug 10%	Sep 9%	Oct 11%	Nov 9%	Dec 7%	TOTAL 100%	ACTUAL
Plbg Svc. Revenue	152,426	163,279	154,000	154,000	176,000	198,000	198,000	220,000	198,000	242,000	198,000	154,000	2,200,000	2,207,705
Maintenance agreements	204	508	490	490	560	630	630	700	630	770	630	490	7,000	6,732
Total Revenue	152,630	163,787	154,490	154,490	176,560	198,630	198,630	220,700	198,630	242,770	198,630	154,490	2,207,000	2,214,437
Cost of Goods Sold														
Labor	46,739	43,664	37,078	37,078	42,374	47,671	47,671	52,968	47,671	58,265	47,671	37,078	529,680	545,928
Materials	38,598	9,205	32,443	32,443	37,078	41,712	41,712	46,347	41,712	50,982	41,712	32,443	446,387	446,387
SPIFF's	10	90	30	30	30	30	30	30	30	30	30	30	360	400
Other	0	0	154	154	177	199	199	221	199	243	199	154	2,207	1,898
Total Cost of Goods Sold	85,347	52,959	69,705	69,705	79,659	89,612	89,612	99,566	89,612	109,519	89,612	69,705	995,717	994,613
Gross Profit	67,283	110,828	84,785	84,785	96,901	109,018	109,018	121,134	109,018	133,251	109,018	84,785	1,211,283	1,219,824
Overhead														
FICA/MED	6,369	7,757	6,484	6,484	6,484	6,484	6,484	6,484	6,484	6,484	6,484	6,484	77,806	78,966
FUTA	655	120	66	66	66	66	66	66	66	66	66	66	798	1,435
SUTA	1,089	987	682	682	682	682	682	682	682	682	682	682	8,184	8,896
Other payroll expense	1,498	1,673	1,620	1,620	1,620	1,620	1,620	1,620	1,620	1,620	1,620	1,620	19,445	19,371
Supervisor	900	244	448	448	448	448	448	448	448	448	448	448	5,372	5,624
Corporate	328	326	357	357	357	357	357	357	357	357	357	357	4,281	4,224
Health Insurance Expense	5,796	5,276	6,516	6,516	6,516	6,516	6,516	6,516	6,516	6,516	6,516	6,516	78,179	76,232
Insurance Expense	2,563	4,045	4,136	4,136	4,136	4,136	4,136	4,136	4,136	4,136	4,136	4,136	49,636	47,968

Each month when you review a budget versus actual spreadsheet, you can see whether you are ahead or behind the yearly budget based on actual numbers. Take action based on what you see. If you are six months into the year and you are way behind budget, the question needs to be asked: how do we make it up so that we meet budget, or do we need to change the budget?

If your company is six months into the year and the company is way over budget in terms of revenue and profit, the question needs to be asked: what are we doing right, or do we need to change the budget?

QuickBooks can't show you this information based on how they report budgets on your P&L statements. You need more detail to manage the company properly.

Revenues should be reported weekly.

Does entering actual data into a budget take more time than just looking at numbers on a QuickBooks report? Of course.

Taking the time to enter the numbers gives you a much better picture of where the company is financially each month. Then, you can take action—keep doing what you are doing well or determine why your expenses might be ahead of budget and take action to correct the overages in expenditures.

16

Not Giving Employees KPIs

||||||||||||||||||||||||||||||||||||||

"I hate annual reviews."

I frequently hear this statement from owners and managers. Most put off annual reviews until they absolutely have to be done or don't do them at all.

Why?

The most frequent answer? "All they care about is how much more they are getting an hour. They don't care what the review says. They leave either happy or pissed off."

If you hate performance reviews too, then it's time to change how you do them. First, every employee should have key performance indicators (KPIs), which define their responsibility in your company. What are they responsible for? What will they be measured on? What is the baseline acceptable performance? What happens if they exceed their KPIs? Are there bonuses?

KPIs are communicated weekly or at least monthly. Then, the annual performance review should not be a surprise to anyone.

More thoughts about performance reviews:

- If you hate doing them, your employees will hate receiving them. Your attitude affects their attitude. Find a way to be positive about the review process.
- Reviews should *never* be a surprise. All employees should know their KPIs and weekly or monthly performance. If you communicate KPIs only once a year, then it probably is a surprise.
- Reviews don't have to include raises. Performance reviews are just that—performance reviews. Raises for great performance or

cost of living can be separate. Many companies do cost of living raises each January.

- Reviews should be based on KPIs. What are the minimum performance metrics for their job? What happens if they exceed these metrics? This is where the raises or bonuses come in.
- Salespeople have quotas and required closing rates. These are their KPIs.

Employees should always know this as well as the bonuses for exceeding these minimum KPIs. Bonuses don't have to be money. They can be time off, too.

Communicate KPI results frequently. When you do this, reviews are never a surprise and they are much more pleasant for everyone.

17

Having a Warehouse Supermarket

||||||||||||||||||||||||||||||||||||

What does your warehouse look like (if you have one)?

A warehouse supermarket is when employees have unlimited access to the warehouse. Nothing is locked. Employees can take anything they want, when they want, whether or not they need it. They have a shopping cart with no cap on spending. They can fill it to their heart's content.

An employee says, "I think I may need this," so off the shelf it goes. Or "The drawings say I need 10 boots, I'd better take 12 just in case." Or "I'd also better take an additional box of flex duct…just in case." Does any of it ever come back? Rarely.

Another employee says, "I used a motor; I'd better take two for my truck, just in case I need it this weekend." And when you inventory their truck, there are thousands of dollars of inventory, some of it damaged from being thrown around in the truck.

In a warehouse supermarket environment, you give your employees the run of the warehouse with a blank check. They don't even think twice about taking the materials and tools they *might* need. They don't have to pay the bill. They think, *The owner can afford it!*

Stop running a supermarket warehouse. Limit access to the warehouse. Have a materials list for projects. Pull the materials from that list. It takes a little time to reset procedures, and you will encounter resistance from field labor who are used to having a free rein. If it takes a parts runner or a warehouse person to accomplish this, then hire that person. It is easy to pay for that person in increased productivity and decreased material expense.

Lock up your warehouses. Lock up your parts rooms. Lock up your tools. It's the best way to save your hard-earned cash.

18

Ignoring Mistakes and Warranty Problems

|||||||||||||||||||||||||||||||||||||||

"You have a warranty problem."

I said this to the owner, and the bookkeeper said this to the owner. It was obvious to us that there was a huge warranty and callback (mistakes) expense.

It fell on deaf ears. The owner ignored us for months. The problem got worse.

The bookkeeper and I knew that the owner only looked at the bottom line of the company's P&L (until he realized that his balance sheet was more important), so I told the bookkeeper to change the order of the expenses on the profit and loss statement.

Warranty and callback expenses then appeared right before the bottom line.

The bottom line value didn't change. Only the categorization of where the expenses appeared changed.

Finally, the owner noticed the huge callback and warranty expenses. These issues soon disappeared, and the bottom line increased.

It's OK to move expenses around on your profit and loss statement as long as the bottom line doesn't change. Sometimes this is what it takes for an owner to pay attention to a problem.

Once attention is paid to a problem, it usually gets fixed.

Track warranty costs and mistakes as a separate expense line (or department) on your profit and loss statement. If you don't, they may get buried and cause unprofitable projects and an unprofitable bottom line.

Operating on the Sell-Produce Curve

|||||||||||||||||||||||||||||||||||||||

"We ran out of work."

You never want to hear this statement.

Most times it happens because your company is operating on the sell-produce curve.

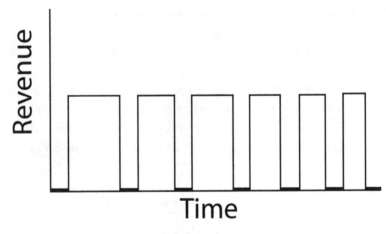

Figure 3. Sell-produce curve

Sell-produce curves generally happen to lifestyle businesses and smaller businesses, as tool businesses don't have a dedicated sales force.

Companies that operate on the sell-produce curve sell until they win a project. During the time they are selling, the company is not producing revenues. When the company wins a project/job, it stops selling to produce the products. Then, when the project is finished, the next project is not lined up, so the company is selling again.

Always have some level of sales and marketing activities when in production. This way the next project will be waiting when the first one is done (see Figure 4).

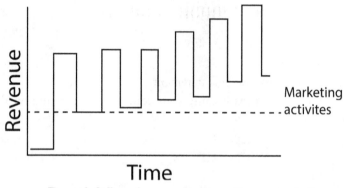

Figure 4. Sell-produce curve with continuous marketing

With continuous marketing, the company is generating sales even when it is producing products. Then, when the current project is completed, another one is usually ready to be performed. Revenues do not drop to zero because the company is waiting to win another project.

20

Running Out of Materials

||||||||||||||||||||||||||||||||||

A $6 roll of duct tape actually cost $252.50!

An installer ran out of duct tape during the installation of a job. He went to his truck. He couldn't find a roll of duct tape. So, he came back to the office. No duct tape in the warehouse. He went to the supply house and purchased a roll of duct tape. Yes, just one roll of duct tape! Then he went back to the customer's home to finish the job.

Unbelievable, but true. This is the calculation for how much this roll of duct tape actually cost the company:

- Stop work. Look in his truck. Travel back to the office: 45 minutes.
- Search the warehouse for a roll of duct tape and visiting with office personnel: 15 minutes.
- Travel to the supply house: 30 minutes.
- Get roll of duct tape at the supply house (and of course check out the latest tools): 30 minutes.
- Travel back to the job: 30 minutes.

Total travel time: 2 hours and 30 minutes.

The installer's wage is $23/hour. Overhead cost is $28/hour.

Direct cost for the duct tape trip = 51 × 2.5 = $127.50

Then he lost 2.5 hours of productivity on the job. The job went into overtime because of the duct tape trip. So, the company had to pay an extra 2 hours of overtime to complete the job that day and get the customer air conditioning in her home.

Additional job cost:

Overtime wage is $34.50/hour. Overhead cost is still $28/hour.

Overtime cost for the duct tape trip: 62.5 × 2 = $125.

Total cost for the duct tape = $127.5 + $125 = $252.50.

You might argue that the overtime overhead per hour is slightly less. However, there still is overhead cost for those hours. The point is that it's expensive to run out of materials.

Make sure employees have all the materials they need to perform work.

Don't let a $6 roll of duct tape cost your company over $250!

21

Not Tracking Revenue-Producing (Billable) Hours

||||||||||||||||||||||||||||||||||

"I don't understand why we are not making money."

A company owner was perplexed. His pricing was right (he thought). The jobs were profitable, according to his calculations. Yet, the company overall was barely making a profit.

It turned out that the revenue-producing employees were productive only about 50% of the time.

That meant that 50% of their time was an overhead expense. The company was paying their employees to do nothing! And this nonproductive time was not included when projects were estimated.

It was a shock to the owners. However, once they saw what they were paying, things changed.

They made sure they had billable work for the employees.

When there was nothing for them to do, they went home (in the past the employees would come to the office in the morning and at the end of the day to "fill their time" for the day).

The owners also had a contest for billable hours (see Mistake 14). Billable hours increased. Revenue increased. The company's net profit increased.

In fact, each employee gets a small quarterly bonus for maintaining billable hours over a certain percentage.

22

Having an Advertising Budget That Isn't Based on Results

||||||||||||||||||||||||||||||||||||

This is a conversation I had with a client who approved and executed an advertising campaign:

"We spent $11,000 on advertising and we only budgeted $5,000."

"So?"

"That's a lot of money to spend. I'm over budget."

"How much revenue did you generate from the advertising?"

"More than $50,000, and we're still getting sales."

At this point he became really quiet. The light bulb went on. He realized that the advertising had worked, and that the $11,000 was a great investment even though it was over budget.

My next question: "Are you going to do it again?"

"Yes, of course. Why wouldn't I invest $11K to generate $50K? This is incredibly profitable for us."

He got it. Invest the advertising money in this way until the investment becomes unprofitable. The original budget doesn't matter. Results do.

Track your results. If the advertising is working, continue the marketing messages until they don't produce enough profitable results, even if you hadn't budgeted to spend that much. The results tell you that the budget in this case doesn't matter. If you end up spending $110,000 and generate $500,000 in profitable sales, keep going, even if your initial budget was $5,000.

Implementing a Marketing Program before You Know It Is Profitable to Do So

||||||||||||||||||||||||||||||||||||

Before investing company funds on marketing and advertising, calculate whether that expense could be profitable. Whether you advertise in the newspaper, on television, through your website, direct mail, social media, or other advertising medium, you should make that investment with an estimate of what results are required for that advertisement to be a good use of money.

The calculations are very simple. Here's how to estimate whether the investment may be a good investment.

Use the following example from Ruth's Rules (see Mistake 32).

What is the break even expense of sending 1,000 postcards, including design of the postcard, printing, and mailing costs?

Take the cost and divide by your gross margin for that department.

Assume the cost of the postcards is $0.50 each (including mailing). The gross margin of the department is 55%. Mailing 1,000 postcards costs $500.

The break-even revenues that must be generated are $500 / 55%, or $909.09.

If you are advertising a product that generates $89 each, then you must generate 10.21 of these items. At 11 items you earn a profit.

Can you generate 11 items from 1,000 names? That is a 1.1% return. The answer is maybe. It depends on who you are sending the postcards to and the offer on the postcards. If you are sending the postcards to people in your database who have not done business with you in the past few years, then the answer is probably yes. If you are sending the 1,000 postcards to a zip code where you haven't done much business, then the answer is probably no. You're likely to get a 0.5% return or less on this type of mailing.

Here's another example: You are paying your web services company $1,500 per month to maintain your website. The gross margin of your company is 45%. What is the break-even amount that must be generated from your website each month to cover the cost of the website maintenance?

The breakeven sales that must be generated is $1,500 / 45%, or $3,333.33 per month. To be fair, look at an entire year because of potential seasonality. The breakeven sales volume from your website is $40,000 per year. Can your website produce these revenues?

The only way to answer this question is to track where your leads and sales are coming from. If a new customer contacts your company, you must ask the question: "How did you find out about us?" Or "How did you hear about our company?"

If the customer says a web search, then you track the dollars generated from that customer and attribute them to the website.

So, before you make any advertising purchase, determine whether the results are likely to at least break even on that purchase.

$$\boxed{24}$$

Not Building a Recurring Revenue Program

||||||||||||||||||||||||||||||||||||||

"Your business is worth only about $100,000."

Unfortunately, I had to tell an owner that his business was worth only about $100,000 after he had invested more than 40 years of hard work. Why? He didn't have many assets or a loyal customer base in a recurring revenue program. He had thought that maintenance plans (this industry's recurring revenue program) were not important. As a result, he had almost nothing to sell.

Recurring revenue programs build a loyal customer base who purchase from you every month, every quarter, or every year. These programs give your customers a reason to talk about your company's products to their family, friends, neighbors, and colleagues.

Every business, whether lifestyle, tool, or transformation, should have a recurring revenue program. It is especially important for lifestyle businesses that can build their entire business around customers who consistently purchase every month, quarter, or year. For tool businesses and transformation businesses, the larger the recurring revenue program, the more valuable the company is. So, the company is worth more when it is time to sell.

Recurring revenue programs generate predictable sales and cash. This cash can be used to support your lifestyle, fund overhead, and build cash reserves.

Determine what your company can provide to your customers on a monthly, quarterly, or annual basis.

Give them a reason to join your program. Think about the benefits that gym memberships, Netflix, Amazon Prime, paid software support, or home/business maintenance programs for lawn care, plumbing, heating, air conditioning, etc. provide.

The recurring revenue program could be free, like a restaurant diner's club where customers earn points toward free appetizers, meals, desserts, and so on. It could have a monthly investment (like your gym membership, Netflix membership, or "Widget of the Month" club). It could have several levels with more benefits at higher price points. It could have a yearly fee, such as software support or Amazon Prime membership.

Ask your customers, create and build your program, and entice your customers to join. They will become your loyal customers. You can achieve your lifestyle and business goals with a strong and growing recurring revenue program.

With a strong recurring revenue program you can be your own bank. Every month, when you receive the monthly billing revenue, deposit that revenue in an interest-bearing savings account. This decreases your company's dependence on a bank line of credit. These funds accumulate quickly and can be your source when you are short of cash. Pay the interest to yourself rather than the bank!

25

Not Having a Referral Program

||||||||||||||||||||||||||||||||||||

"I would appreciate your giving these to the owner. I'm in the plumbing and heating business and would appreciate your business and your colleagues' business."

This is what one of my clients said to the manager of the restaurant where we were having dinner as he handed the manager two business cards.

My client gets referrals and new work this way. He's never afraid to ask for business.

What restaurants do you frequent? What other businesses do you buy from? These are all potential clients.

Referrals aren't the cheapest form of advertising. That distinction belongs to business cards. However, referrals are the best form of advertising. Why? Because one of your customers has talked with a friend, colleague, relative, or neighbor about their positive experience with your company. This person listened to your customer and expressed a similar need (or remembered your company when they did have a need from the story your customer told). Your company gets a phone call. Assuming their experience is positive, your company gets a sale. Your company got this sale without having to spend precious dollars on media advertising.

Some people just give referrals and don't want anything for them. Others want to be incentivized for giving your company leads. In either case, having a strong referral program will help you generate leads and sales with a leg up against your competition.

Referral sales are usually easier sales. A level of trust has already been established because your company did a great job for that person's friend or neighbor. Your company's proposal could also be higher than some competition, but you got the sale because it was a referral.

Google reviews, Yelp reviews, and website testimonials help your referral program. Video testimonials should be on your website.

Most people do a web search when they discover they have a need. They want to find out about specific types of equipment, companies, and stories. Your testimonials from customers tell a positive story about your company. These are crucial, and, if someone doesn't know anyone, the web search can be the reason that they call your company.

Referral and reminder programs can be passive or active (that is, subtle or overt). A passive program means that you don't make announcements about your referral program. You just surprise a person with flowers, a thank-you note, or some other thing. You hope that surprise encourages that person to continue to refer people to your company.

An active referral program is a conscious effort to tell all customers that you have a referral program, what that program is, and what they can expect if they participate in the program. Some customers will choose to participate, and others won't. These programs usually offer gift certificates or cash.

Announcements of the program can be as simple as information on the back of a business card, or it could be announced in a newsletter or a special mailing to your customers.

Here are two referral stories.

Company 1's salesperson did a great job, and the price was right, but they did not get the sale. When the salesperson asked why they lost the project, the customer was honest with him. She told him that it was a difficult choice because she and her husband liked both proposals. They liked Company 1's salesperson. Both salespeople did everything right. The decision was made to go with the other company because they had a referral from a colleague.

Company 2 decided to give $50 for every lead that was referred to the company. The owner didn't expect much but made a commitment to mention it to every customer they did work for. The first month he got eight leads and sold six. And, in two of the cases, his price was higher. He discovered that one of the main reasons he got the projects even though his price was higher was because they were referrals. The referral program expanded exponentially, since those who had initially referred his company continued to do so. And the referrals referred others, and so on. His comment after a few months was that the $50 was a very inexpensive lead cost and he wished he had started it sooner.

Referral programs don't have to be complicated. They just have to be consistent. That means that if it is verbal, the salesperson mentions it at the end of every project. The office personnel need to know about it so that if a customer calls they can explain it to that person. In addition, give everyone in your company the same opportunity to earn a referral fee as your customers. They'll start referring customers to the company too.

26

Not Knowing Where Your Leads Are Coming From

|||||||||||||||||||||||||||||||||||||||||||

This mailer didn't work was the thought of an owner until he went to a service meeting.

He made the expressed the thought during the meeting. Everyone said it did work and they were getting the blue postcards with the $25 off coupon.

The mistake? Not tracking where the leads were coming from.

If you don't know where your leads are coming from, you don't know whether to continue an advertising program or stop it (see Mistake 22).

If your friends say they saw you on TV or heard you on the radio, it's *not* an indication that your advertising programs are working. The exception to this is if they buy your products as a result of hearing the advertising.

Your employees must ask why someone contacted your company. Was it a referral, a web search, hearing a radio advertisement, seeing a commercial on TV, or something else? If your prospective customer says they came to you via a web search, ask, "What prompted you to click on our website?" Many times the answer is they heard an ad, saw a commercial, etc.

The best way is to to ask, "How did you hear about us?" Pay attention to the answer and record it somewhere. Many times your software programs can do this by assigning a specific telephone number to a specific advertising campaign. Run the report on that telephone number, and you will discover how many calls that advertising campaign produced.

Then track to see how much revenue was generated as a result of those leads. And, if the advertising source isn't generating leads, stop wasting the company's money!

27

Not Tracking Revenue-Producing Employees' Average Sale

||||||||||||||||||||||||||||||||||||||||

"I was shocked. Our most senior technicians have the worst average revenue."

This was the first time that the company had looked at how much each technician was producing in terms of revenue per service ticket. The manager was shocked to discover that the less experienced technicians actually had the highest average revenue. Since they were going to start posting average revenue per service ticket, the manager realized he couldn't do it without embarrassing the most senior technicians with the longest tenure at the company.

He decided to bring each technician in to the office and show that technician their revenue as compared to others in the department (all names were eliminated). Each technician was given ideas on how to increase their revenue. They discussed the fact that by explaining to customers things that could help them be more comfortable in their homes and offices, they were actually helping customers by educating them. They were also told that in three months the revenue per truck for all employees would be posted each month.

This worked. None of the most experienced technicians wanted to be embarrassed. They brought their average service ticket revenue in line or higher than the less experienced technicians.

As a result of posting the numbers, everyone's revenue increased. The customers were better taken care of and the bottom line of the department increased.

Most employees like to know how they are doing in relation to others in their department. Make sure that your most tenured employees are not the least productive. If they are, then give them ways to become more productive. Then, explain that the numbers will be posted each month so that everyone can see how they are doing. This usually becomes a competition among your employees to see who has the highest numbers.

Then consider giving bonuses to everyone who reaches a certain goal each month.

The customers become better educated, the employees get more income, and the company gets a better bottom line.

28

Not Tracking Salespeople's Closing Rate

||||||||||||||||||||||||||||||||||

"I didn't realize he was burning leads."

A manager was reviewing quarterly results for his three salespeople. All received 30 leads. He discovered that Salesperson 3 was the least profitable even though their closing ratio was the highest among the three. They were dropping the price so they could get the sale and their commission.

The company distributes leads equally among three salespeople. Table 3 shows the results for one period. Closing ratios don't tell the whole story. The person with the highest closing percentage might not be your best salesperson.

Salesperson 3 has the highest closing ratio and the smallest average sale. Salesperson 2 has the highest sales volume and the lowest closing ratio.

The sales volume is equal for Salesperson 1 and Salesperson 3 even with Salesperson 3's closing ratio.

TABLE 3. SALESPERSON RESULTS

	Salesperson 1	Salesperson 2	Salesperson 3
# of proposals	30	30	30
# of closes	10	8	20
Value of closes	$20,000	$32,000	$20,000
Average sale	$2,000	$4,000	$1,000
Closing ratio	33%	27%	67%

In terms of dollar value of the sales, Salesperson 2 is the highest even though they have the lowest closing ratio.

Go one step further. Which salesperson has the most profitable sales? (Table 4).

TABLE 4. SALESPERSON PROFITABILITY

	Person 1	Person 2	Person 3
Average sale	$2,000	$4,000	$1,000
Gross margin	40%	40%	40%
Gross profit	$800	$1,600	$400
Overhead cost per sale	$50	$50	$50
Net operating profit	$300	$1,200	-$600

Salesperson 2 is the most profitable even though they have the lowest closing ratio.

Salesperson 3 is losing money for the company on every sale. They should not get a commission on unprofitable sales. The directive to Salesperson 3 was "Get your minimum average sale to $2,000 even if your closing ratio decreases. The company will not pay commission on sales that don't make a profit."

29

Not Firing a Customer

IIIIIIIIIIIIIIII|IIIIIIIIIIIIIIII

"We're going to go out of business…but we don't care if we do."

This is what three partners said to each other when they went through their entire customer base and decided who to fire. It was the end of their fiscal year, and they were really tired of doing business with some of their customers who were costing them money. These customers:

- Always complained.
- Always wanted a discount.
- Didn't pay their bills without collection calls or were notoriously 60 to 90 days or more late.
- Were rude to their employees.

In one case, the building that their employees went to was unsafe.

Once they got through making the list, they were firing about 10% of their customers. This made them nervous, but they were resolved to do it.

They fired them with ruthless compassion. What does this mean? They met with each customer they were firing and explained that they were not going to do their projects the following year. They gave these fired customers a list of potential companies who could do their projects.

What happened?

To their surprise, profits actually increased the following year. They realized that they weren't spending time with unprofitable customers and they could spend time with profitable customers.

As a result, at the end of every year, they review their customer list and decide who, if anyone, they are going to fire. The list was never as long as it was the first year.

The thing that really surprised them was that around the third year, several of the fired customers called asking if they could come back. The owners said yes, as long as the customer paid their bills on time, didn't complain, and so on. These customers realized how well this company took care of them and hadn't found another company who performed as well as they did.

Never be afraid to fire unprofitable customers. It doesn't make sense to keep a customer that you pay to do their projects (that is, their net profit per hour is negative).

30

Not Putting GPS on Your Vehicle Fleet (Where It Is Legal to Do So)

IIIIIIIIIIIIIIII|IIIIIIIIIIIIIIIII

"You were speeding."

"Officer, no, I wasn't."

"Yes, you were. Here's a traffic ticket for speeding."

This is the conversation between an employee with a GPS tracker in his truck and a police officer who pulled him over. The employee knew he wasn't speeding. The manager pulled the GPS report on his vehicle, which proved he wasn't speeding, and took it to court. Case dismissed. The employee was thrilled that he was right and there would be no points on his driving record.

The Global Positioning System (GPS) allows you to track the movement and behavior of an employee driving your company vehicle. You always know where your vehicles are as long as the GPS is mounted somewhere it always stays on.

First, check with the laws in your state. Some states, like Tennessee, have laws pertaining to the use of GPS tracking devices in vehicles. Other states require that you get a signed statement that the employee acknowledges that there is a tracking device in the company truck.

Almost every company owner with a fleet that employees drive installs GPS trackers where it is legal to do so. The cost of installation and maintenance usually pays for itself in a few months with the reduction of fuel costs. The only employees who complain are those who abuse the use of the trucks: they use them without permission on the weekends and go places they shouldn't be.

GPS tracking is a safety issue. I've seen GPS trackers save lives—an employee passed out in his truck and went into a ditch (thankfully he didn't hit anyone and survived). When he didn't get to his location, the dispatcher saw the location of his truck, called 911, and sent a manager to help him.

GPS trackers prove that your employees were at a specific location and how long they were there. Sometimes customers call saying that an employee was not at their location as long as the time stated on their invoice. Or, in other cases, the travel time gets questioned. GPS tracking can tell a customer when the employee arrived and how long they were there. This resolves a customer complaint easily.

Dispatchers and other employees who schedule the fleet drivers can keep an eye on where the employees are and when they move. Employees can be routed more efficiently, saving fuel costs as well as giving the employee the potential to generate more revenue in a day.

31

Ignoring Ruth's Rule 1:
How Much Revenue Has to Be Generated
by a Direct Cost Employee?

||||||||||||||||||||||||||||||||||||||||

I developed Ruth's Rules many years ago to calculate the revenues needed for any expense, whether a cost of goods sold expense or an overhead expense.

Ruth's Rule 1 is used when a candidate for a direct cost of goods sold position (that is, one who generates revenues for your company) says, "I want $X per hour."

Your answer should be "Fine. Can you generate Y per hour?"

You determine Y using Ruth's Rule 1:

Sales = Direct Expense / (1 – Gross Margin)

Gross margin is a percentage.

Here's how to use Ruth's Rule 1: You are considering hiring a new cost of goods sold employee who has great experience and wants $40/hour. The gross margin of this department is 52%. Benefits are 30% of wages, and truck cost is $10/hour (USA average). Assume 2,080 hours a year.

- Wages = $40 (2,080) (1.3) = $108,160
- Truck cost = $10 (2,080) = $20,800
- Total cost = $128,960
- Revenues needed = $128,960 / 0.48 = $268,666.70

Can the employee generate $268,667 a year? If the answer is yes, then their $40/hour is justified.

Do this calculation for any direct cost employee. If a person wants $30/hour, calculate how much that employee has to generate to pay the $30/hour.

Each cost of goods sold employee should know how much revenue he has to generate to pay his hourly wages. Consider a bonus for exceeding those revenues.

32

Ignoring Ruth's Rule 2:
Are You Generating Enough Revenue to Break Even on an Overhead Expense?

||||||||||||||||||||||||||||||||||||

Ruth's Rule 2 is:

Sales at Break Even = Overhead Expense / Gross Margin

Here's how to use Ruth's Rule 2: Your training expense is $1,000 a month. What is the breakeven revenue that has to be generated assuming your company gross margin is 55%?

Sales at Break Even = $1,000 / 0.55 = $1,818.18 a month

Now that you know the breakeven revenues that have to be generated, look at the revenues that are generated as a result of an employee who attends training class. Do they add at least $1,818.18 a month as a result of the training? If so, then you are fine. If not, then what can you do to get the revenues to this volume?

Here's another way to use Ruth's Rule 2: Your office manager, who has been doing a great job, wants a raise from $50,000 to $60,000 a year. What increase in revenues does the company need to have assuming the company gross margin is 35%?

The additional expense is $10,000 (for simplicity, don't include payroll taxes and other benefits).

Sales at Breakeven = $10,000 / 0.35 = $28,571.43

To justify their raise, ask them how they will help the company increase revenues by $28,571.43.

33

Ignoring Ruth's Rule 3:
Are You Generating Enough Revenue to Make a Profit on an Overhead Expense?

||||||||||||||||||||||||||||||||

Assuming that you want your company to be profitable, rather than just break even, use Ruth's Rule 3:

Sales = Overhead Expense / (Gross Margin – Profit)

Gross margin is a percentage, and the profit you desire is a percentage.

Here's how to use Ruth's Rule 3: Your office manager asks to go to a training class. The class tuition is $1,000. It is two days and their salary is $3,000 a week. Your gross margin is 45%, and you want a 15% profit. What are the revenues that have to be generated as a result of them attending the training?

Class Cost: $1,000

Wages Cost: ($3,000 × 2) / 5 = $1,200

Total Cost: $2,200

Revenues needed: $1,200 / (0.45 – 0.15) = $4,000

Here's another way to use Ruth's Rule 3: You are hiring a new office person. Their salary is $20/hour plus 30% benefits. The gross margin of this department is 48% and you want a 10% net profit. What are the revenues that the company has to generate to pay her wages?

Total salary including benefits: $20 ⊡ 2,080 ⊡ 1.3 = $54,080

Sales = $54,080 / (48% – 10%) = $142,315.79

Can you increase revenues by $142, 315.79? If the answer is yes, then hire that person for that position.

34

Not Having a Buy-Sell Agreement with Partners— Even If the Partners Are Family Members

‖‖‖‖‖‖‖‖‖‖‖‖‖‖‖‖|‖‖‖‖‖‖‖‖‖‖‖‖‖‖‖

Here's why partnership agreements are necessary, even for family members:

Three siblings own and operate a company. Each sibling has their area of expertise and is good in that area. They make joint decisions about the direction of the company. Each trusts the other two siblings to do their job well. They all have check signing authority on the company bank accounts.

One of the siblings, who was responsible for the financial side of the company, got hooked on drugs. The other two siblings knew this sibling had a drug problem. But, they had been promised by this sibling that she had "kicked the habit." Unfortunately, this wasn't true.

This sibling slowly started taking money out of the business checking account to fund her drug habit. It wasn't caught by the other two siblings until they started having cash flow problems.

Here are the four steps they took:

First, when they discovered the theft, they immediately took their sister's check signing privileges away. This meant going to the bank and signing new signature cards. No more money got siphoned out of the company for drug purchases.

Second, they removed check temptation from their sister. They put the checks in another location she didn't know about, under lock and key, unless they were being used. In this case, they also had to remove her from the financial side of the business and insisted that she go to a rehabilitation facility. They hired a bookkeeper.

Third, they told her that she no longer had check signing authority and the signature cards have been changed.

Fourth, the other siblings became more involved in the financial side of the business. They also kept an eye on cash. Had they done this before their sister got hooked on drugs, the problem would have been caught more quickly, before the cash flow problems began. The bookkeeper provided weekly cash flow reports, and one of the siblings checked the bank accounts each day.

Thankfully they also had a buy-sell agreement in place in case something like this happened.

Had there not been a buy-sell agreement in place, it would have been difficult to get her out of the company, even though her actions were detrimental to company operations.

It wasn't fun to buy out their sister's shares and kick her out of the company. But you must get a buy-sell agreement in place, even with family members.

Also, all partners should always keep an eye on cash, even if a trusted sibling has the day-to-day financial responsibility.

35

Not Knowing Why You Are in Business

||||||||||||||||||||||||||||||||||

If you don't know why you are in business and you are unhappy, your business probably won't be profitable long-term. If you're unhappy and you have employees, they can sense that you are unhappy, and most won't stick around for long. Most lifestyle businesses and transformation business owners know why they are in business and enjoy life as a business owner most of the time. The tough businesses are tool businesses—these owners generally go through tough times as they grow to use their business as a tool to fund their goals.

If you are miserable quit, get out, sell your business, and do something that makes you happy. Life is too short to be miserable.

Here's another way to look at it.

I attended a workshop hosted by Morgan James, the publisher of my books *The Courage to Be Profitable*, *Profit or Wealth*, and this one. Jim Howard, the COO and publisher for Morgan James Publishing, presented a session on building a business that ROCKs. I found Jim's presentation to be a useful reminder of how to build a profitable, sustainable business that you enjoy:

R: What is your reason for being in business? Why are you doing this? The key question, according to Jim, is, what does your customer get out of it? Your reasons have to be big enough for your customer and you to care.

O: What is your offer? What are you providing them that they want or need? Their wants may be different than their needs. Many of us get what we want rather than what we need. People buy on wants and justify the need later.

C: Communicate. How do you tell them about your offerings? What pain are you going to fix? You must control perception. According to Jim, you can't build it and they will come as they did in the movie *Field of Dreams*. You have to build it and tell them they need it.

K: Keep them. How do you keep them? My answer: recurring revenue builds stable cash flow and loyalty. You are loyal to them, and they become loyal to you when they trust you.

||||||||||||||||||||||||||||||||||||

Dumb Mistakes:

Pricing

||||||||||||||||||||||||||||||||||||

These are mistakes that business owners make when pricing their products and services. Making these mistakes causes unprofitable bottom lines.

36

Pricing Incorrectly

||||||||||||||||||||||||||||||||||||||

The correct way to price is to start at your desired net profit per hour and work backward from the bottom of your profit and loss statement.

Most companies determine what their direct costs are and then divide by 1 minus the gross margin. This does not take overhead into consideration. (see Mistake 31).

Start at net profit. What net profit do you want to earn for each project? Do you want a higher net profit for projects with higher equipment cost? Do you want a lower net profit for projects with a higher labor cost?

These are questions you need to answer before you establish your pricing.

One of my clients continually complained about a particular type of labor-intensive projects. He moaned that he could never make money on them because of the labor involved.

I said, "Fine. What net profit per hour do you want for those projects?"

He answered, and then we established the prices for those jobs.

He agreed that if a customer was not willing to pay what he required to do those projects, then he would not do the work.

I never head a complaint about those types of jobs again.

To price properly, start at the bottom line.

1. What net profit per hour do you want to earn?
2. What is the overhead cost per hour?
3. Add the two numbers. This gives you your gross profit per hour.
4. How many hours will the project take?

5. Multiply those hours by the gross profit per hour. This gives you your total gross profit.
6. Then add the direct cost for the job. (Make sure you add commission in these numbers.)
7. This is the selling price to the customer.

To determine the cost for one hour of labor:
- Your desired net profit per hour: $75/hour
- Your overhead cost per hour: $40/hour
- Your highest-wage employee: $35/hour

Net profit	$75
−Overhead	$40
=Gross Profit	$115
Direct cost	$35
Selling price	$150

This assumes you can bill all 2,080 hours of this person's labor.

If you can only bill 1,500 hours, then you must take unbillable time into the rate:

$$150 * 2,080 / 1,500 = \$208/\text{hour}$$

Your billing rate would be $208/hour using these assumptions.

Not Realizing That Growth Masks Pricing Issues

|||||||||||||||||||||||||||||||||||||||

Would you knowingly buy a part for $1 and sell it for 93 cents?

Of course not!

However, if you are running your business based on how much cash your company has, then this can happen. The first story in this book describes two business owners who were losing a nickel for every dollar they took in the door for 12 years.

They didn't intend to sell at a loss. However, without checking that they were actually making a profit and relying only on the cash they had, they were lulled into a false sense of security.

When you are rapidly growing, your cash is increasing rapidly, too, as long as you are collecting for the work you perform quickly. Without accurate tracking of costs and accurate financial statements, you'll never know whether you are buying a part for $1 and selling it for 93 cents.

A five- or seven-cent loss is hidden by the rapid increase in cash. However, cash is growing a nickel or seven cents less for every dollar collected than it should be growing. You can't see it unless you track costs and prepare accurate financial statements.

Accurate financial statements are critical to ensure that prices are correct.

Thinking Cash and Profits Are the Same Thing

||||||||||||||||||||||||||||||||||||

"I made a profit—where's the cash?"

You look at the bottom line of your profit and loss statement every month and see that your company has a profit. You see profits month after month, yet you run up against a cash crunch: needing cash for payroll or having to pay your taxes, or another major use of cash.

You just don't understand how your company can be profitable and you don't have cash.

Here's the answer: profits are just that—profits. It means that your revenues were greater than your expenses. A loss happens when expenses are greater than revenue. Neither means that you have cash. Profits are a P&L item. Cash is a balance sheet item. The two are very different.

So, how do you get cash? Here is the detailed explanation: a revenue (P&L) turns into an accounts receivable (balance sheet) when you bill for the work you did. Then you must collect for the work you did (balance sheet). If you operate on COD, your accounts receivable instantly turns into cash (balance sheet). When you get vendor invoices you enter them as an expense (P&L) and create an account payable (balance sheet). Then you must pay your account payable (balance sheet) and hopefully you have cash left (balance sheet).

Some companies experience months when the company showed a loss, yet there is still cash in the bank. The opposite is also true: there are times where the company shows a profit and you are having problems scraping enough cash together to pay payroll.

Warning: Even though your P&L shows a profit month after month, you can grow your company out of business. This happens when you run out of cash (see Mistake 10) and don't have a line of credit or recurring revenue savings to cover temporary cash shortages.

Here are five specific ways to go broke:

1. Doing profitable work and collecting for it months later or never collecting for it. You still paid your employees and your suppliers.

2. Not job costing (see Mistake 89) so you can make sure that your projects are sold at a profitable price.

3. Using the cash method instead of the accrual method of accounting (see Mistake 7).

4. Performing profitable work but the client files bankruptcy during the middle of a project, leaving your company with hundreds of thousands of dollars in receivables that are uncollectable.

5. Purchasing too much inventory, giving your employees total access to your warehouse, and allowing them to keep too much on their trucks (see Mistakes 17 and 57).

Profits don't pay the bills. However, collecting the cash from profitable jobs is necessary to pay the bills. Collect for your profitable work quickly, pay your bills associated with that job, and stay solvent.

39

Pricing Using Markups

||||||||||||||||||||||||||||||||||||||

"We're making 35% on all of our parts sales."

"How are you determining that?"

"We mark them up 35%."

"You're not earning 35%. You're only earning 26%."

"Huh?"

This was the conversation I had with a new client. The explanation I gave him is below.

The best pricing is using net profit per hour (see Mistake 36).

However, many companies use the markup method of pricing, which is the most dangerous way to price, because markups are based on cost and don't correlate to your company's gross profit and gross margin.

Here is the difference between markup and margin and why pricing by markup can hurt your bottom line:

You want to earn a 40% markup or a 40% margin on a part that costs $10.

Using the markup pricing method:

$$\$10 * 1.4 = \$14$$

You charge $14 for that part.

Using the margin pricing method:

$$\$10 / 0.6 = \$16.67$$

(See Ruth's Rule 1, explained in Mistake 31.)

You charge $16.67 for that part.
Here are the calculations:

	Markup	Margin
Revenue	14.00	16.67
Direct cost	10.00	10.00
Gross profit	4.00	6.67
Gross margin	28.5%	40%

You're only earning 28.5% on a markup of 40%.

If you're not willing to price using net profit per hour method, then use the margin rather than markup pricing method. It's a better indicator of what your costs really are.

40

Not Understanding Direct Costs

|||||||||||||||||||||||||||||||||||||||

"Our gross margin is 60%. We're doing really well."

"What costs do you have in direct costs?"

"Just labor and equipment."

"You're missing a lot of cost that should go in direct cost."

This is the conversation I had with a business owner who didn't really understand cost.

What did I mean?

Direct costs or cost of goods sold are costs incurred when you produce revenue. Many companies just include labor and equipment to produce a product or service. This is only part of the direct cost that should be shown on your profit and loss statement.

Overhead costs are costs incurred to stay in business. These include rent, utilities, and so on—costs that must be paid whether or not you produce revenue.

One of the biggest mistakes is not including commissions in direct cost. Commissions are not paid unless a sale is made and revenue is produced. Therefore, it is a direct cost.

Another is forgetting credit card charges or financing fees. You don't incur these costs unless you sell a product and a customer pays for it by credit card or finances the project.

Finally, you might have costs for shipping, permits, and warranties (see Mistake 50).

All of these costs go into direct costs, which lowers your gross profit and gross margin.

If you are pricing on the gross margin method rather than net profit per hour (see Mistakes 36 and 39), including these costs will increase your sales prices to the customer.

Why? Because your gross margin will be lower and your costs will be higher.

Here is an example of two prices. One price includes $1,000 direct cost without commission and financing fees. Once commission and financing fees are added to direct cost, the cost is $1,200 and the gross margin drops to 38%. Using the 1 – Gross Margin pricing method, the two sales prices are below.

	Cost	Gross Margin	Sales Price
No commission and financing fees	$1,000	40%	$1,666.67
Commission and financing fees	$1,200	38%	$1,935.48

Make sure you put all of your direct costs in cost of goods sold so your customer gets an accurate proposal price.

41

Assuming Each Project Should Have the Same Overhead

IIIIIIIIIIIIIIIII|IIIIIIIIIIIIIIIII

This is the conversation I had with a client when discussing how to price.

"How do you account for overhead when pricing your projects?"

"We assign a 35% overhead factor to all of our projects."

"That is absolutely the wrong way to price."

"Why?"

"Let's look at two $10,000 projects. One has 16 hours of labor, and the other has 100 hours of labor. Right now each job gets $3,500 in overhead cost assigned to it, right?"

"Yeah."

"Tell me how it is fair that one project that has more than triple the labor cost has the same overhead as the other project."

Dead silence. Then, "You're right. The job with more labor should have more overhead assigned to it. What do I do to fix it?"

"Price using overhead cost per hour. Each billable or revenue-producing hour is assigned the same amount of overhead. Let's assume that your overhead cost per hour is $40 an hour."

"OK."

"Here's why. The 16-hour project gets $640 in overhead cost. The 100-hour project gets $4,000 in overhead cost. You'll lose money on the 100-hour project."

"Got it."

Each project should get overhead assigned to it based on the number of labor hours for that project. Don't reward high-labor jobs with low overhead dollars, and don't penalize low-labor projects with high overhead.

42

Allocating Overhead Incorrectly

||||||||||||||||||||||||||||||||||||||||||

Departmentalization must be fair to each department.

If you do not have different departments, then to calculate your overhead per hour, get your total overhead cost from last year's fiscal year end profit and loss statement. Divide that number by the number of revenue-producing labor hours last year.

For companies with different departments, then you must departmentalize overhead. Each department must get its fair share. Calculate departmentalized overhead based on space costs and labor costs, because they are the two components that create overhead.

How do you do it fairly? How do you do it so that each department gets its fair share of the amount of overhead that should be allocated to that particular department?

Some companies departmentalize by sales volume. This probably isn't fair, because it's rare that two departments with the same sales volume have equal numbers of employees producing that sales volume.

Here are two department's revenues and number of employees.

	Department A	Department B
Sales	$1,000,000	$1,000,000
Revenue-producing personnel	2	8

Department B will have more overhead simply because it takes more people to support Department B than Department A (more billing, phone calls, customers, etc. to produce the $1,000,000).

If you calculated overhead based on sales in this scenario, Department A and B would get equal overhead allocations. But Department B should receive a higher overhead allocation because it has more revenue-producing personnel that require more office support than Department A.

Overhead is caused by space expenses and people expenses.

Here's how to calculate overhead so each department gets its fair share.

First, the space overhead. There are five things that cause space expenses: rent, utilities, building maintenance, building taxes, and building insurance. Determine the total amount of revenue-producing space used by each department. Revenue-producing space is the space occupied by either people or things related to a revenue-producing department. Common areas, such as a conference room, kitchen, and bathrooms, are not included; bookkeeping space doesn't count; your reception area doesn't count. The space that is used by financial people or other people who are not producing revenues do not count in this equation. The only area that counts is the space related to your departments.

Next, people overhead. Every overhead item not included as space overhead is related to people. For example, the more people you have, the more office supplies you have. The more people you have, the more telephone calls you have.

Calculate people overhead by using the total direct labor cost for each department. Then take the percentages of the total company direct labor cost as the percentage of people overhead each department should incur.

If you know the exact amount of time that somebody spends in a particular department, then take that percentage rather than the overall estimate shown in this example. If you have a bookkeeper who is splitting her time between three departments determine how much time she is spending in each department on its tasks and then allocate her salary appropriately. For example, assume your bookkeeper's salary is $50,000 per year and she spends 20% of her time in Department A, 30% of her time in Department B, and 50% of her time in Department C. Then,

Department A gets $10,000 of her salary, Department B gets $15,000 of her salary, and Department C gets $25,000 of her salary.

If materials or services are bought only for one department, then that department gets 100% of that expense. For example, advertising or printing. Many times advertisements are placed for only one department. As such, that department receives all of that advertising expense. For website expenses, divide the expense by the revenue-producing payroll percentages. It's hard to determine if a department should get more or less of that expense.

Once you know the total amount of overhead for each department, then calculate the overhead cost per hour by dividing each department's overhead by its billable labor hours.

Usually, you get an eye-opening experience the first time you calculate your overhead costs per hour for your company and each of your departments. At first, you may be estimating some of the overhead costs. Make the best estimates you can. Then, refine the costs as you increase productivity and get more exact with each overhead item. You will get more and more accurate each year you calculate your overhead cost per hour.

Table 5 is an example of a company with three departments.

TABLE 5. OVERHEAD COST PER HOUR CALCULATION EXAMPLE

	Department 1	Department 2	Department 3	Totals
Occupied space (sq. ft.)	2,000	3,000	5,000	10,000
Space	20%	30%	50%	
Billable labor	$250,000	$500,000	$750,000	$1,500,000
Labor	16.7%	33.3%	50.0%	
Billable labor (hours)	6,000	8,000	25,000	39,000

Overhead Expenses				
Direct department expenses	$20,000	$10,000	0	$30,000
Space expenses	$60,000	$90,000	$150,000	$300,000
People expenses	$166,667	$333,333	$500,000	$1,000,000
TOTAL EXPENSE	$246,667	$433,333	$650,000	$1,330,000
Overhead/hour	$41.11	$54.16	$26.00	$34.10

Not Knowing Your Overhead Cost per Hour

||||||||||||||||||||||||||||||||||||||

"This department is unprofitable."

An owner was shocked when he looked at overhead for three company departments and his favorite department was unprofitable. Here are his results:

	Dept 1	Dept 2	Dept 3
Overhead/hour	$22.32	$31.89	$100.27

"How do I get the overhead cost per hour down?"

My answer: by having as many revenue-producing hours as possible. For example, if you pay an employee for eight hours but he only can bill a customer for four hours, you'll have a higher overhead cost per hour. Another way to reduce your overhead cost per hour is to ask your employees. They know how they waste time. Many times you have to ask the office about the field operations and vice versa. They know. Implement their suggestions.

Finally increase the number of revenue-producing employees in Department 3. This means growing the department.

The owner implemented the suggestions, and the overhead cost per hour dropped significantly. This resulted in more profit for that department.

Comparing Business Bottom Lines on Percentages Rather Than Net Profit per Hour

|||||||||||||||||||||||||||||||||||||||||

"I made a 10% net profit this year."
   "So did I."
   "We both did well."
   Which owner was really more profitable?
   They both had a 10% net profit. They both had the same number of billable hours.
   However, when comparing the two businesses on a net profit per hour basis, Business B was a much more profitable business.

	Revenue	Net profit	# billable hours	Net profit per hour
Business A	$1,000,000	$100,000	3,000	$33.33
Business B	$1,500,000	$150,000	3,000	$50.00

They utilized their labor hours better. They produced $50 net profit per hour, whereas Business A only produced $33.33 net profit per hour.
   True business comparisons are on a net profit per hour basis. Percentages don't tell the real story.

Paying Commissions on Based on Gross Margins

IIIIIIIIIIIIIIIIII|IIIIIIIIIIIIIIIII

"The minimum gross margin for commission is 40%. We pay a commission on any project with a 40% or higher gross margin."

This company may be paying commissions on jobs that lose money. The is the rule for commission payment for salespeople in a company until they learned about net profit per hour.

Here is the job cost analysis for two jobs, each over 40% gross margin.

	Sell price	# of hours	Gross profit	Gross margin	Overhead	Net profit	Net profit / hour
Job 1	$12,903	39	$5,227	40.51%	$2,348	$2,879	$73.34
Job 2	$5,644	59	$2,273	40.27%	$3,552	-$1,279	-$21.37

Both jobs had a 40% gross margin. One job earned $73.34/hour net profit. The other paid the customer $21.37/hour (it lost money).

This shocked the client. They couldn't imagine two jobs, each with the same gross margin, where one made a profit and the other a loss.

The salespeople didn't care. They made their commission whether or not the job actually earned a profit. In the second case, the salesperson won and the company lost. It's important that everyone wins or everyone loses. That's fair.

In Job 2, the sales person grossly underestimated the number of hours on the job. He estimated based on achieving a 40% gross margin. The actual selling price should have been at least $6,922.96 to break even (net profit would be zero).

Paying commissions on gross margins is dangerous because gross margins don't tell the whole story. Pay commission after overhead is calculated in job cost to ensure the job made a profit before you pay a commission.

The best way to pay commission is through net profit per hour. The company owner decides the minimum net profit per hour that the company has to earn, and anything over that number is the commission paid to the salesperson (up to a maximum net profit her hour).

For example, assume the company wants to earn a minimum of $50 net profit per hour and a maximum of $100 net profit per hour. In this case, the salesperson for Job 1 would receive a commission of based on 39 hours and the difference between $50 minimum net profit per hour and the $73.34 that the job earned. The commission would be (73.34 − 50) × 39, or $910.26.

The salesperson for Job 2 would receive no commission.

Of course, if there were issues outside of the salesperson's control, such as price increases after the proposal was accepted, then the salesperson would not be penalized for these increases in costs.

Paying through net profit per hour rather than a percentage eliminates "salesperson estimated hours" versus real hours to do the job. Salesperson estimated hours are always lower that the real hours to do the job because they want a low price to win the work and get their commission.

Unprofitable Pricing Discounts

||||||||||||||||||||||||||||||||||||||

"I need to have a sale because I need to generate revenues. I'll discount the prices by 30% to entice people to buy now."

This was the thinking of a business owner. Was his price discount OK? Could he still break even on sales with this discount?

Here are the details:

- Normal price is $97.
- Cost of goods sold is $39.
- Gross profit is $58.
- Overhead is $30.
- Net operating profit is $28.

With a 30% discount, the price is $29.10 less, or $67.90.

Cost of goods sold and overhead remain the same.

Net operating profit is –$1.10. The company loses on each sale. So if it sells 100 products, the loss is $110.

This company owner got a huge influx in sales. Unfortunately, he learned after the sale that the discount was too steep.

He discovered that if he had lowered the price to $77 instead, which would have probably resulted in similar sales, that the company would have made a small profit rather than a loss.

Before you offer discounts, make sure that discount doesn't cause that product's sales to be unprofitable after overhead is taken into consideration.

Not Including Parts Waste/Shrinkage in Pricing

||||||||||||||||||||||||||||||||||||||||

"We only use half a sheet of wood in a product."

"What happens to the rest?"

"We scrap it."

"How do you price?"

"By using the half sheet cost."

My next question was whether the rest of the sheet could be salvaged. It couldn't because of the way the half sheet was used.

This owner realized that the entire sheet of wood should be in the price because he couldn't salvage the other part of the sheet. As a result, the price increased slightly and his net profit per hour increased dramatically.

Heating and air conditioning contractors also see this waste when they purchase flex duct for installation of the homes. The cost must include the entire box of flex (or more than one box depending on the amount needed) since the remainder of the box gets scrapped most of the time. Those contractors who calculate cost with the exact amount of flex needed often lose money because they pay for the whole box and only cost the part of the box used in the construction.

Rule of thumb: If you use part of a product and can't use the rest, include the whole product in the direct cost. This makes your gross profit an actual gross profit because you included the cost for shrinkage.

Not Realizing Labor Is Like a Hotel Room

||||||||||||||||||||||||||||||||||||||

What do I mean? Labor, like a hotel room, is perishable.

If a hotel owner does not sell a room today, he has lost because the ability to sell that hotel room that day is gone forever. Tomorrow he has the opportunity to sell that room again. If he does, he has revenue. If he does not, then he's lost that ability to earn revenue that day for that room.

Labor is also perishable. If you don't sell a person's labor today, then it is lost. You cannot sell that labor tomorrow.

Inventory is different. If you don't sell it today, it sits in your warehouse or on your truck and you can sell it tomorrow.

Labor that is not sold is gone forever. The unbilled hour or unbillable day is irreplaceable.

On average, employees work 40 hours a week or 2,080 hours a year. Assuming you deduct for vacation, holidays, meeting time, and training time, you can only sell about 1,900 hours a year. About 91% of the employee's time can be sold—that is, billed.

How many hours a year per employee do you actually sell?

Your pricing must include the cost for those hours you cannot sell.

Track billable or sold hours against the number of hours you paid an employee. That is your sales or billable percentage.

Let's assume your billable percentage is 80%. If an employee earns $50/hour, then he actually costs $50 / 80%, or $62.50/hour. And, if your overhead cost is $40/hour, then the $40/hour also has to be divided by 80% because overhead is based on billable or sold hours.

The actual breakeven cost for the employee is $62.50 + $50 ($40 / 80%), or $112.50.

Make sure you consider the hours you can't sell in your pricing.

Labor is a precious commodity. Profitably sell all the hours you can sell.

49

Not Considering Unbillable Hours in Pricing

||||||||||||||||||||||||||||||||||||||

If you pay an employee for 2,080 hours a year (not including overtime), then you have to account for the number of hours that are not billable in your pricing.

For example, most companies have an employee benefit of a minimum of one week's vacation, six holidays, and potentially other hours for additional vacation or holidays. The minimum is 88 hours (40 hours for vacation and 48 hours for holidays).

In addition, most companies have meetings or send their employees to training throughout the year. Let's assume this is an additional 40 hours.

In this case, the number of unpaid hours is 128 hours for benefits plus training/meetings.

These hours must be accounted for when setting prices. They cannot be directly billed to the customer, yet they must be paid for.

Here's how to ensure your company is included these types of hours in your pricing.

When you calculate the price to the customer, the labor cost is 40 hours at $30/hour for a total of $1,200. You must add the unbillable hours divisor.

$$128 / 2,080 = 6.2\%$$

The divisor is 93.8%.

So, the labor cost should be $1,200 / 0.938 = $1,279.32.

The $79.32 difference may appear to be minimal. However, the costs add up. How many projects do you have in a year that will lose $79.32? This goes directly to your bottom line.

Always account for non-revenue-producing labor hours in your pricing.

50

Forgetting Warranty Costs in Pricing

||||||||||||||||||||||||||||||||||||||

"Our warranty costs are eating our lunch!"

"What's going on?"

"There's a recall from the manufacturer, and we have to install a new part. The manufacturer is supplying the part and telling us we have to supply the labor. It's really expensive."

"Did you put any warranty cost in your pricing?"

"No. How much should I put in?"

The answer to this question depends on your yearly warranty costs. This was an extreme case with a product recall and replacement. But the company didn't have a warranty reserve on their balance sheet to take care of this issue.

Generally the warranty expense added to proposal estimates is 1% to 2% of material/equipment costs. However, it is best to calculate your warranty costs for the previous few years and divide that into the equipment/material costs to get your percentage.

How do you account for the warranty cost?

Whatever the cost is, debit warranty cost in cost of goods sold and credit warranty reserve on your balance sheet. Then put the dollar value of the warranty cost in a savings account (debit the savings account and credit your operating account).

If there is a warranty claim, then debit warranty reserve for amount of the claim and credit warranty revenue for the same amount. The warranty expense should match the warranty revenue, so the gross profit is zero.

For example, assume that equipment material cost is $10,000. These are the journal entries:

Warranty reserve is 2%, or $200.

Cost of goods sold – warranty expense = $200

Warranty reserve = $200

A warranty claim of $150 is submitted.

Warranty reserve = $150

Warranty revenue = $150

The profit and loss statement would look like this:

Warranty revenue = $150

Warranty cost of goods sold = $150

Gross profit = $0

There is still $50 in warranty reserve to cover any additional warranty claims.

Two hundred dollars might not seem like a lot of money. However, multiply the $200 times the number of projects you perform in a year. The warranty reserve and your savings account should have a lot more than $200. You won't get a warranty claim on every project. You will be prepared to handle the few warranty expenses you do incur.

51

Different Employees Pricing Differently

||||||||||||||||||||||||||||||||||||||||||

"I got a cheaper price six months ago from Dave. When Steve gave me a proposal for the same thing it was $2,000 higher. What's going on? I want Dave's price."

A customer service representative got this call. And no, the difference was not because of inflation. It was because Dave and Steve priced differently.

Upon investigation, this was typical. Dave always priced lower than everyone else in the company. Why? He wanted the commission and artificially lowered the price so that he would win the work.

In this case the customer forgot that Dave had given her a proposal six months prior. When she called to get a price, then Steve gave her a much higher one. She thought it was too high and found Dave's original proposal.

All employees must price the same way. The best way is through a pricing book or pricing software. There are hundreds of software options. Choose one that fits your needs.

Then, everyone prices using the same process and arrives at the same price unless they are playing games with the software. Managers should review the discounts or changes in costs and take appropriate action.

If prices change because of inflation, that is easily explained. However, if employees or salespeople price so that they get the project, then you may have unprofitable work.

Many times there are salesperson hours and real hours. Salesperson hours are always lower than the real number of hours needed to complete a project. This happens when salespeople are paid on gross margin rather than net profit (see Mistake 45).

52

Not Raising Prices When Costs Increase

"I got a quote a year ago. Can I get the project done for the same price?"

This was a question that a potential customer asked the salesperson who gave him the quote.

The salesperson checked the proposal and realized that prices had increased 30%.

He called the customer back and said, "Unfortunately our prices have increased 37% (including raises to their employees). The new price is $X."

The customer was shocked but needed the project done. He agreed to the increased price.

What would have happened if the salesperson said yes?

The company would have lost money on that project. The salesperson wanted his commission, which was based on net profit, so he told the customer that prices have increased and gave him a new price. If he had kept the price the same, he would not have gotten a commission.

The company made the same bottom line dollars as the year before.

There have been huge price increases in the past few years. You must increase your prices to stay even. The mistake in thinking is that you can maintain your sales prices. If you do, your bottom line suffers and you earn less for the same amount of work.

When you hold your prices constant as costs increase, your company is spiraling downward toward unprofitability.

The spiral often continues until costs increase so much that your company becomes unprofitable. Of course, in the beginning your company gets more sales because other companies have increased their prices to cover their increases in costs and customers flock to your door because your prices are cheaper.

Then, you get more unprofitable sales until you grow yourself out of business. (Remember the story at the beginning of this book. When growth stopped, cash flow problems began.)

If you get a price increase, you have to increase your prices to your customers. In addition, you may have to increase your prices because you gave raises to your employees to keep up with the rate of inflation. If you increase wages by 5%, remember that you'll be paying additional payroll taxes, so prices must increase at least by 6.5% to cover the additional benefits costs (assuming a 30% benefits cost).

In addition, all proposals should have a "this proposal is good for 30 days" statement at the bottom. This gives you an out if prices have increased.

|||||||||||||||||||||||||||||||||||||

Dumb Mistakes:

Balance Sheet

|||||||||||||||||||||||||||||||||||||

This section describes dumb balance sheet mistakes that, if ignored, could put your company in a cash flow crunch or put it out of business.

53

Not Recognizing That Your Balance Sheet Is More Important Than Your P&L

||||||||||||||||||||||||||||||||||||||||||

"I never look at my balance sheet."

This is a common statement from many business owners.

Most owners, unless they are a CPA or bookkeeper, don't start their business to do the financial part of business. Yet reviewing and understanding financials helps keep companies in business.

Understanding and reviewing balance sheets are the least understood financial concepts. Yet, they are the most important.

Your balance sheet shows you true profitability. Your profit and loss statement shows profits for a month or a quarter or a year. Then, it starts over. Your profit and loss statement doesn't show you continuous profits.

Unfortunately, many small business owners never look at their balance sheets. They don't understand what they are saying, so they ignore them. They only look at their P&L. Balance sheets tell you true profitability, over a long period of time. A P&L only tells you whether you made a profit for a month, quarter, or year.

Your balance sheet also answers the questions:

- Can you pay your bills?
- Are you taking on too much debt?
- Do you have too much inventory?
- Do you have a collection problem?

When reviewing financial statement each month, looking at both the balance sheet and P&L statements is essential so you can spot minor issues and take care of them before they become major crisis.

54

Having a Balance Sheet That Doesn't Balance

IIIIIIIIIIIIIIIII|IIIIIIIIIIIIIIII

"Never give me a balance sheet that doesn't balance."

"You know how to read these statements?"

"Yes."

This was the conversation between an upset owner and his new bookkeeper. The bookkeeper had prepared the financial reports and given him a balance sheet that didn't balance. This was a test by the bookkeeper (we think) to see if the owner knew how to read them. Thankfully he did.

The definition of a balance sheet is that assets must balance liabilities and net worth (capital or equity).

If your balance sheet doesn't balance, this is a warning sign that something is very wrong. Most software packages don't allow a debit entry without a corresponding credit entry. This is the accounting software's safeguard that a balance sheet will balance.

However, one-sided journal entries are permitted in some software. This means that a debit can be entered without a credit, and vice versa. Unbalanced balance sheets occur when this happens. Embezzlers use this to embezzle.

If you ever have a balance sheet that doesn't balance, then you must investigate immediately. Discover what's wrong and fix it.

Having Negative Cash on Your Balance Sheet

|||||||||||||||||||||||||||||||||||||||

Unfortunately, I see this too often.

You cannot have negative cash in the bank. That means the bank owes you money or your account is overdrawn. The bank doesn't owe you money. If your account is overdrawn too often, you'll experience huge check charge expenses and the bank will close your account.

The cash flow tank shown in Figure 2 (see Mistake 9) is a visual representation.

There can never be less than a drop of money in the tank. Negative money is *not* possible.

So, how do you get negative cash on your balance sheet?

The most common way is for bookkeepers to print out all the payables due and hold the checks until there is money to pay the bills. At the end of the month, the bookkeeper is still holding checks.

Your accounting system doesn't care. It just requires that debits match credits. The bookkeeper has paid the bill by printing the checks, and the accounting system takes the cash to pay the bill even if there is not sufficient cash to cover the bills.

Never write a check unless there is money in the account to cover the payment. This will eliminate negative cash on your balance sheet.

The unfortunate second way this happens is through embezzlement. You don't pay attention to your balance sheet and don't question why there is negative cash.

It's easy to hide unauthorized payments to anyone this way. Someone can write a check out of QuickBooks, print it, and delete it in the software. Yet, it is a printed check that can be cashed. When the bank statement is reconciled (which it should be monthly), the cash balance on the balance sheet should be negative. If you don't see the reconciliation report, you have no idea whether it was reconciled properly and the numbers match the balance sheet.

In addition, owners should sign all checks. Unless the check is forged or it is written to a similar-sounding company and you don't catch it when you sign it (which is a possibility), a bookkeeper could not embezzle this way because you would question the check. Similar-sounding names would be, for example, ABC Company and ABC, Inc. These are potentially two different companies: one your legitimate vendor and one owned by the embezzler.

56

Having No Inventory or the Same Inventory Number on Your Balance Sheet

IIIIIIIIIIIIIIIII|IIIIIIIIIIIIIIIII

"We lost a quarter of a million dollars in net worth in a day."

This happened to a business because it had the same inventory number on their balance sheet for more than two years.

When they finally counted it, the value of inventory was $250,000 less than the value stated on their balance sheet. The business was worth $250,000 less than it was the day before.

How does this happen? Don't pay attention and don't track inventory.

What was the loss per employee per day?

Here's how the loss was calculated:

$250,000 a year for two years is $125,000 a year.

Divide $125,000 by 52 is $2,403.85 a week or $480.77 a day.

There were 32 employees who touched inventory, so that is just $15.02 a person a day. It's easy to lose, damage, or steal $15.02 a day.

If your company uses materials and equipment in the performance of your work and you purchase these materials for use later, then you must account for inventory purchases and inventory use on your financial statements. This is the only way to know true profitability.

Why?

If all materials go into cost of goods sold even though some are inventory, you are increasing your costs and your bottom line is less than it should be.

However, if you're a lifestyle business and you are the only one touching inventory, this matters less because you know what you buy and you know what you use. It is unlikely that you'll be in a situation where someone is stealing inventory because you are the only one who uses it.

For tool or transformation businesses, tracking inventory is critical. You don't want to end up with loss, damage, or theft decreasing the value of your business.

And inventory is a bet.

Walk through your warehouse. How many parts are gathering dust on the shelves? How many parts did you buy a year ago or more that you paid for but still haven't used?

Inventory is one of the greatest cash drains for small businesses. You are betting your hard-earned dollars that you will be able to sell something that you've bought for a "good deal."

57

Not Looking at Inventory Days Trends

|||||||||||||||||||||||||||||||||||||||

Know how many days, on average, it takes from the time you purchase a part until you use it in your products and services. If it is over 30 days, you probably have too much inventory unless your business is parts distribution.

Track this number through inventory days. (Inventory turns are used to calculate inventory days.) If your company does not have inventory, do not calculate this ratio or the inventory days ratio.

Inventory days is the number of days between the time a part is purchased and the time it is used to create a product or provide a service.

First calculate inventory turns. Inventory turns are calculated on annualized costs. Calculate this ratio by using both the profit and loss statement and the balance sheet. It is calculated:

Annualized Material Expense / Inventory

or

Annualized Cost of Goods Sold / Inventory

For construction companies, I calculate the ratio on cost of goods sold rather than just material expense. The reason is that for the construction industry, labor is an integral factor in inventory usage. It is rare to find a company that can install or service a part or piece of equipment without labor expense.

To annualize material expense or cost of goods sold, take the year-to-date material cost or cost of goods sold times 12 and divide by the month of the fiscal year you are in. So if you're in month 7 of your fiscal year, take the year-to-date cost of goods sold times 12 and divide by 7, and that's the number to divide the inventory into.

Can seasonality affect this ratio? Perhaps. Since you are annualizing the sales or cost of sales, then the annualization is not seasonal. The important thing is to look at the trends and see what is happening with the ratios. The ratios might be higher after a spring or fall stocking order. However, you'll notice this year after year and come to expect it.

Inventory days is a financial ratio that measures the average time a part is in your warehouse before it's used. Calculate this ratio from the inventory turn number. It is calculated:

365 / Inventory Turns

If inventory days are increasing, this is a warning sign. There is more purchasing or less usage, or perhaps stocking orders issues.

Inventory is a bet. Don't stock more than you think you can reasonably sell. Be very wise and thoughtful in how you purchase inventory. You are betting your hard-earned dollars that you will be able to sell it. I have seen a lot of bad bets over the years with obsolete inventory.

If you have decreasing inventory days, you have less purchasing or more usage. That's exactly the trend you want to see until inventory days stabilize at a certain number. You want the lowest reasonable inventory levels. Obviously it's expensive for an employee to visit a supplier every five minutes. You need a reasonable level of inventory that you can turn or that you can use in a reasonable amount of time.

One more thing to watch: if your company has inventory, look at receivable days to inventory days. Receivable days (see Mistake 71) should always be greater than inventory days. If you have 30 days of receivables and 60 days of inventory, you have twice as much inventory as needed. Drop the days down to 30 days and save a lot of cash.

If these figures are out of line, then it is also possible that the inventory figure is overstated or understated (when was the last physical inventory taken?) or the company has parts that are unusable. In either of these cases, the unusable inventory should be written off or a physical inventory should be taken to determine the true inventory level.

58

Putting Long-Term Assets/Liabilities in Current Assets/Liabilities

IIIIIIIIIIIIIIIII|IIIIIIIIIIIIIIIII

"I don't get it. My current ratio is over three. Why am I having a hard time paying my bills?"

This owner had a false sense of security (see Mistake 68). Actually, his current ratio was under one when he took out the owner receivables from the current assets. He actually had a hard time paying his bills!

Current assets are assets that are cash or turned into cash within a year. Examples of current assets are cash, accounts receivable, inventory, and prepaid expenses.

Long-term or fixed assets are assets that are not turned into cash within a year. Examples of long-term assets are furniture, computers, equipment, vehicles, and buildings.

Current liabilities are liabilities that must be paid within a year. Examples of current liabilities are accounts payable, credit cards payable, taxes payable, lines of credit, current portion of long-term debt, and deferred income.

Long-term liabilities are liabilities that the company has that are longer than a year. Examples of long-term liabilities are vehicle loans, equipment loans, mortgages, and other bank loans.

One of the biggest mistakes is with owner receivables and payables. If you lend the company money or take money from the company as a loan and you or the company are not planning to pay it back within a year, those loans should be in long-term liabilities or long-term assets.

When you review your financial statements, you need to know whether you actually have enough current assets to pay your current liabilities. Putting long-term assets in current assets or putting long-term liabilities in current liabilities might give you a false sense of security that you can pay your bills.

59

Not Collecting Your Accounts Receivable

||||||||||||||||||||||||||||||||||||

"Our employees can't get gas in their trucks today."

This company had over $1 million in receivables and didn't have enough cash in the bank to pay the late fuel bill.

It was a wake-up call for the owners.

"We're too busy to collect" was the excuse I was given until the day that they needed fuel for the vehicles and didn't have enough money in the checking account to pay the fuel bill.

Finally, getting cash in the door became important. Collecting became a part of the bookkeeper's job every week.

They never had a collection problem again.

Of course, companies that collect COD, such as retail stores and restaurants, should never have a collection problem.

Think of collecting past due accounts as the fulfillment of a contract, whether written or implied. Your company agreed to provide a product or service. The customer agreed to pay. Your company fulfilled your part of the contract. The customer has to fulfil its part of the contract.

If your company's payment terms are net 30, on the 31st day someone must call to inquire about when you will receive payment. This is a friendly call. It sends a message to the customer who owes your company money that you are serious about collections.

If you don't get paid when your customer says you would, then you must make another call.

In some cases, you'll ask when you can pick up a check. This is another way of being serious about collections.

Your company did the work. It's your customer's responsibility to pay you on the terms you negotiated.

$$\boxed{60}$$

Having Negative Accounts Receivable on Your Balance Sheet

||||||||||||||||||||||||||||||||||||||

Negative accounts receivable means that your company owes your customers money. While you may owe a few customers a refund, you don't owe your entire customer base a refund. On an aged accounts receivable report, you may see a few negative numbers for those customers you owe refunds to. The entire aged receivables list should not be negative.

Generally, negative accounts receivable happens because you got a deposit for sold work that has not been billed. The bookkeeper erroneously enters the deposit in accounts receivable. Since an invoice has not been generated, the accounts receivable is negative.

Deposits for work that has not been performed are liabilities. They go in the current liabilities section of your balance sheet under a deposit account.

When you perform the work and invoice the customer for the work, the deposit is applied to revenue (debit the amount of the deposit and credit revenue). The total invoice for the work performed less the deposit is the accounts receivable amount.

For example:

You receive a $10,000 deposit on a $100,000 project.

The journal entry is:

Cash = $10,000

Current liabilities – deposits = $10,000

When the project is completed and billed to the customer:

Accounts receivable = $90,000

Current liabilities – deposits = $10,000

Revenue = $100,000

This keeps accounts receivable an accurate, positive number on your balance sheet.

61

Not Comparing the Accounts Receivable Aging Report to the Accounts Receivable Balance on Your Balance Sheet

IIIIIIIIIIIIIIIII|IIIIIIIIIIIIIIIII

"Someone is stealing from you. Your accounts receivable reported on your balance sheet doesn't match your accounts receivable total on your aging report."

"Why don't they match?"

"Let's look at your journal entries."

The journal entries showed accounts receivable credits and cash debits through ACH withdrawals. That's why the accounts receivable value on the balance sheet didn't match the accounts receivable aging report.

The bookkeeper was stealing through accounts receivable. She would make journal entries through accounts receivable rather than the accounts receivable software module. As a result, the value reported on the balance sheet never matched the aging receivables report. The cash went to her through ACH withdrawals, so the owner never saw a check. Since she balanced the checkbook, she could check off the withdrawals without anyone seeing them.

An accounts receivable aging report should be given to you along with a profit and loss statement and balance sheet at the end of every month. Check to make sure the total receivables amount matches the amount shown on your balance sheet.

If they don't match, start investigating. Even if they match, check the journal entries made. There should be very few journal entries. Each journal entry made should also have an explanation as to why that entry had to be made. Most of the time, entries are made through one of the accounting modules so that journal entries don't have to be entered.

This quick check is one action to take when you review your financials each month.

62

Ignoring Your Accounts Receivable and Accounts Payable Aging Reports

||||||||||||||||||||||||||||||||||||

"I don't know why we are having cash flow problems. We're busy."

When this business owner finally started paying attention to his aged receivables report, he discovered that several of his customers owed him more than $100,000 that was over 90 days old. He had hired John, an accounts receivable clerk, who, in the beginning, did a phenomenal job. Their accounts receivable days dropped to under 45 days. Their receivable days had not been this low in a long time.

The owner stopped paying attention to the accounts receivable aging report, assuming that John was doing his job.

Months later, his controller told him they were headed for a cash flow crunch. He couldn't understand why, since he assumed John was doing his job well. Surprise! John was not performing.

The owner called the companies that owed money and requested payment. He then requested an accounts receivable aging from John every week. Receivable days started decreasing again.

Every week, when you receive your weekly cash flow report (see Mistake 8), an aged receivables and an aged payables report should accompany it.

Look at it!

See which companies owe your company money and, just as important, who your company owes money to. Pay attention to supplier invoices. You'll be able to quickly tell whether an employee is purchasing materials and supplies in great quantities.

Find out why and if those purchases are justified.

Accounts receivable and accounts payable aging reports are critical to protecting your cash flow.

Not Comparing the Accounts Payable Aging Report to the Accounts Payable Value on Your Balance Sheet

||||||||||||||||||||||||||||||||||||||||

Like accounts receivable values, your accounts payable reported on your balance sheet should match your accounts payable total on your aging report.

Theft of materials is the biggest reason that these two values don't match.

Someone purchases materials outside your accounts payable module. Then the supplier is paid with a check. You recognize the supplier, a legitimate company, but the materials you are paying for are not going through your cost of goods sold materials expense.

An accounts payable aging report should be given to you along with a profit and loss statement and balance sheet at the end of every month. Check to make sure the total payables amount matches the amount shown on your balance sheet.

If they don't match, start investigating. Even if they do match, check the journal entries. There should be very few journal entries made. Each journal entry should also have an explanation as to why that entry had to be made. Most of the time, entries are made through one of the accounting modules so that journal entries don't have to be entered.

This quick check is one action to take when you review your financials each month.

Having Negative Loan Payments on Your Balance Sheet

||||||||||||||||||||||||||||||||||||||

"Has the truck loan payment been made?"

"Yes. Why?"

"The balance sheet says that the bank owes us money for the loan."

"Huh?"

"There is a negative truck loan balance on the balance sheet."

At this point the owner knew that his bookkeeper didn't know bookkeeping.

Negative loan values means that the bank or other creditor owes you money for that asset purchase—not likely.

This is what happened. Whenever a loan payment was made, the entire amount of the payment was debited against the loan amount. But in fact, the payment is a combination of principal repayment and interest.

At the end of the loan period, if the entire loan payment was applied to the principal, it will show a negative amount on your balance sheet. Part of the payment should be interest.

Assume that the truck payment is $500 a month. Of the $500, $100 is for interest and $400 is for repayment of the principal. The journal entry looks like this:

Loan repayment = $400

Interest = $100

Cash = $500

In most accounting software systems, this recurring invoice can be set up with the loan payment and interest as the debit and cash as the credit. Then, you will see the correct balance owed to the bank every month.

65

Having Negative Payroll Taxes on Your Balance Sheet

|||||||||||||||||||||||||||||||||||||||

One of the easiest ways to tell that your financial statements are wrong is to see negative payroll taxes in the current liabilities section of the balance sheet. Negative payroll taxes payable mean that the government owes you money. This is not likely unless you've made a huge mistake.

Here are the mechanics of payroll tax payments as they relate to profit and loss statements and balance sheets.

1. Employees get a certain hourly wage or salary each week. This is a profit and loss expense item—either in direct expense for your field employees or overhead expense for office and officer employees.

2. Employees pay a certain percentage for FICA and Medicare taxes. This is a balance sheet item. You withhold the money on their behalf and pay it to the government every week.

3. Employers match the FICA and Medicare taxes that the employee pays. This is a profit and loss expense item. You get to pay the match to the government every week.

4. Employers withhold other amounts from employees' checks such as income taxes, garnishments, 401(k) payments, etc. These are balance sheet items, not profit and loss expenses.

5. Employers are liable for state and federal unemployment taxes. They are not deducted from employee checks. They are a profit and loss expense item.

This example looks at the payroll entries one at a time. Most payroll companies summarize the entries (for example, federal payroll taxes payable is for withholding and FICA and Medicare).

First, employee Steve's payroll:

- Steve earned $1,000 this week.
- His FICA and Medicare deduction is $76.50.
- Your company matches the $76.50 as a P&L expense.
- His state income tax withholding is $100.
- His Federal income tax withholding is $200.
- He has a child support garnishment of $150 a week.

The journal entries you make into your accounting software:

Wages	$1,000.00
FICA and Medicare payable	$76.50
State Withholding payable	$10.00
Federal Withholding payable	$200.00
Garnishment payable	$150.00
Cash paid to employee	$473.50

Both sides add to $1,000. Notice the only P&L expense is Steve's wages. Everything else is a balance sheet item.

Second, enter the payments you are required to make as an employer:

Employer FICA and Medicare expense	$76.50
FICA and Medicare payable	$76.50
State unemployment tax expense	$20.00
State unemployment tax payable	$20.00
Federal unemployment tax expense	$7.00
Federal unemployment tax payable	$7.00

Expense amounts are P&L expenses. Payable amounts are balance sheet, current liabilities accounts.

When you pay the government taxes and garnishment debit the tax payable or garnishment and credit cash.

Using this method of recording tax expenses and taxes payable generally records positive payable values on the balance sheet.

Incorrectly Accounting for Asset Purchases on Your Balance Sheet

||||||||||||||||||||||||||||||||||||||||||

You purchase a new major tool, truck, building, or other major asset whose value is depreciated over time. This is a long-term or fixed asset on your balance sheet.

If it is a purchase that does not have to be depreciated, you can record the purchase on your profit and loss statement as a tool, supply, office furniture, or other expense.

When you purchase the asset for cash, the journal entry is simple: debit the fixed asset and credit cash.

Incorrect accounting arises when the asset is purchased using a loan.

Assume you purchase a new truck for $40,000. The down payment is $4,000 and the remaining $36,000 is financed for a four-year period.

There are two portions of the liability: the current portion of long-term debt and the remaining long-term debt.

Remember that current liabilities are those payments which must be made in a year. Therefore, one year of the loan is in current liabilities and the remaining three years are in long-term liabilities.

Here are the journal entries when the truck is purchased:

Fixed assets	$40,000
Cash	$4,000 (for the down payment)
Current portion of long-term debt	$9,000 (25% of the value of the loan since it is a 4 year note)

Long-term debt	$27,000

Then, when the payments are made, the principal payments are deducted from long-term debt until the last year of the loan. Current portion of long-term debt remains constant (assuming it is a simple interest loan) until the final year of the loan.

$$\boxed{67}$$

Incorrectly Accounting for Recurring Revenue on Your Balance Sheet

||||||||||||||||||||||||||||||||||||||||

Properly tracking and accounting for recurring revenue plans is critical to the success of your program.

If you bill monthly for recurring revenue programs and provide service/products monthly then there is no deferred revenue.

Deferred revenue only applies if you collect in advance of providing the services. Whether you collect the entire year's payment up front or you collect 1/12th of the payment each month through monthly recurring billing, the dollars you collect are not yours until you perform the work or provide the product. The dollars you collect are a liability to your company. You have an obligation to perform work or provide the product that you have received money for. Your customer paid you on a bet and the faith that you will deliver what they are paying for in advance.

The money you receive should go into an interest-bearing savings account. It should not go into your operating account. This is not your company's money until it does the work! If your customer wants a refund, it should be taken from the interest-bearing savings account.

When your company receives the money, it is accounted for in the balance sheet current liability account called deferred income.

Assume that your customer, Mrs. Jones, paid you $180 for the year. When you receive her payment the transaction is:

Debit Cash – Savings Accounts = $180

Credit Deferred Income – Recurring revenue = $180

Notice that when the money is received it is not a sale, as long as your company is using accrual accounting. You get revenue when you perform the work.

Assume your company provides service twice a year.

- Debit Deferred Income – Recurring revenue for $90 when the first service is performed (balance in the account is $90)
- Credit Sales – Recurring revenue for $90

You have decreased the liability to perform by $90 and increased sales by $90. Then, the cost to perform that work is taken out of the $90 in revenues.

Next, the company performs the second service. The accounting transaction is:

- Debit Deferred Income for $90 (balance in the account is $0)
- Credit Sales – Recurring Revenue for $90

There is no more liability to perform. The customer received everything that was promised. Your company has the total revenue of $180 and $0 deferred income.

What happens to the cash when the work is performed? If necessary, take $90 from the savings account to cover expenses and put it in the operations account. If the cash isn't needed to cover expenses, leave it in the savings account. The dollars build up to provide your company with a cash safety net.

What happens if you record the sale when the customer enrolls in your recurring revenue program? You have financial statement fruit salad (see Mistake 87).

Make sure that you have a deferred income account and a savings account on your balance sheet. Then, record the sale and performance of your recurring revenue program services accurately. You'll know that your profit and loss statements are accurate, and you can see whether you are breaking even or profiting from your recurring revenue sales.

Ignoring Current Ratio Trends

|||||||||||||||||||||||||||||||||||||

"We didn't get our financials for three months, and now we're in a cash flow crunch."

This is the current ratio results for this company, calculated in April (no financials were received for three months since December):

Month	Dec	Jan	Feb	Mar
Current ratio	1.04	1.02	0.99	0.93

In December the company was barely able to pay its bills. By April they were in a huge cash crunch. Had the owner known the ratio decline in January, he could have done marketing to increase profitable sales to avoid this situation.

Paying attention to your current ratio trend alerts you to a potential cash crunch.

Current ratio is a measure of liquidity—that is, how easily can your company pay its bills? It also answers the question, Is your company becoming more or less profitable?

Calculate this ratio by using figures from the balance sheet. The ratio is:

Current Assets / Current Liabilities

Current assets are assets that are cash or turned into cash within a year. Current liabilities are bills that you have to pay within a year. Do not include owner receivables or payables that will not be repaid within a year. Check Robert Morris, Risk Management Association, or Dunn and Bradstreet for the average ratios in your industry.

A current ratio under 1.0 means your company is in a cash crisis. You don't have enough current assets to turn into cash to pay all your current liabilities. The only way to reverse a current ratio less than 1 is continuing profitable sales.

Assume that you calculate the current ratio, and it is 1.95. Is that good or bad? It actually depends. If your standard industry ratio is 1.50, the ratio looks good. However, compare the ratio to your previous month's ratio. If the month before you had a current ratio of 2.05 and it decreased to 1.95 this month, that's not good, because the ratio is trending the wrong way. Or, if the previous month was 1.65 and it went to 1.95 this month, your company is doing better. You are going in the right direction.

With these ratios, you have to look at the trend. A single figure won't tell you too much. Are the ratios going the right way, or are the ratios going the wrong way?

An increasing current ratio because of a cash infusion (think PPP loans) inflates your current ratio. It is not increasing because your company is becoming more profitable.

A decreasing current ratio is the first indication of lessening profitability. If the current ratio is decreasing, 90 times out of 100 that means your profitability is decreasing. You are likely to have a higher percentage of expenses as compared to revenues, which means higher current liabilities as compared to current assets.

The major other reason there might be a decreasing current ratio is you bought a long-term asset. For example, if you paid cash for a vehicle, then you've decreased cash, which is a current asset item, and you increased a long-term asset—a vehicle. So your cash decreased and your long-term assets increased. When cash decreases and current liabilities stay the same, the current ratio decreases. The same thing would happen if the company purchased a lot of equipment, office furniture, or a building using cash rather than borrowing money to purchase the assets. It is converting current assets into long-term assets, which reduces your current ratio.

If your company's current ratio is increasing, then it is becoming more profitable and it has more ability to pay its bills. If the ratio is decreasing, determine why. For example, look at profitability and determine what has to be done to turn profits around. If the current ratio is staying about the same, the profitability is probably staying about the same. Another reason current ratio might increase might be a sale of assets. If a truck was sold, this is transferring a long-term asset (a truck) to a current asset (cash). The current ratio would increase in this situation. However, the main reason, most of the time, that current ratio increases is that profitability is increasing.

69

Ignoring Acid Test Trends

||||||||||||||||||||||||||||||||||||

"We didn't know we were building inventory."

How did they see it? The ratio between the current ratio (see Mistake 68) and the acid test was increasing. The trends for these two ratios should be parallel (see Figures 5 and 6). If the distance between the two ratios is increasing, inventory is being built up in your company.

Current Ratio and Acid Test Trailing Ratio

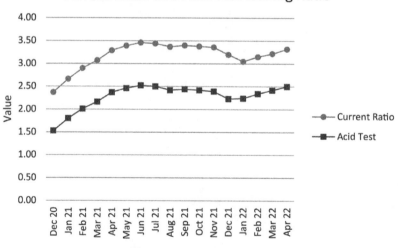

Figure 5. Normal current ratio and acid test trend

The acid test is also called the quick ratio. If your company does not have inventory, you do not calculate this ratio. For those companies that do have inventory, calculating this ratio tells you about inventory usage.

Calculate this ratio by using values from the balance sheet. It is calculated:

Current Assets – Inventory / Current Liabilities

Again, check Robert Morris or the Risk Management Association for the average ratios for your industry. Like the current ratio, if you have a decreasing acid test, you are not as profitable or you bought some assets. If you have an increasing acid test, you are more profitable or you sold some assets. Generally the acid test follows the same trend as current ratio.

If your current ratio is changing and your acid test is staying the same value from month to month, or vice versa, this means that your inventory is changing as seen in Figure 6.

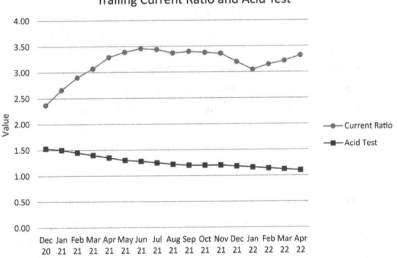

Figure 6. Current ratio and acid test trend when inventory is increasing

If your current ratio is the same and the acid test is decreasing, then you are trading cash for inventory. Be very careful. Inventory is a bet and can drain your cash.

70

Ignoring Debt Trends

||||||||||||||||||||||||||||||||||||||||

There are two debt ratios, debt to equity, and long-term debt to equity.
"Somethings wrong. Our debt to equity ratio jumped."
Below are the values for the debt to equity ratio for this company.

Month	June	July	August
D/E	2.65	2.62	3.02

What made the ratio jump? The company purchasing agent purchased
more inventory than normal. He said he got a great deal if he bought
immediately. Was it a good bet? Yes, fortunately. They were able to sell
more products at higher profit because of lower material cost.

Debt to equity (D/E) ratio looks at the amount of debt that the
company is burdened with. Calculate this ratio by looking at the balance
sheet. It is calculated:

Total Liabilities / Total Equity

Total debt is total liabilities, both current liabilities and long-term
liabilities. Divide total liabilities by the equity (total net worth or capital) of the business. The result should be greater than zero but as low as
possible.

The debt to equity ratio doesn't have "an average value." I've seen
this ratio as high as 11 and the company was still profitable. Most of the
time when the debt to equity ratio increases dramatically several large,
long-term projects are in their initial stages. The company is purchasing

significant quantities of equipment and materials. When this happens, you should also see a high jump in accounts receivable as the company bills for these materials.

If your current ratio and your acid test are moving in the right direction, your long-term debt to equity is in the proper range (which I'll discuss next), and your compensation percentage is within averages, the value of your debt to equity ratio is not that important unless it jumps in a month as in the example above because the company can service the debt—that is, it can pay its bills (see Mistake 90).

So, regard the debt to equity ratio as a warning ratio. It should not jump up or increase rapidly. It should be consistent or decreasing. If it is increasing, that is a warning sign that the company is purchasing a lot of material or may not be paying its bills. A decreasing debt to equity ratio means that profitability is increasing and the company is paying off debt. If the debt to equity ratio is increasing, the company has decreased profitability and is incurring more debt. Watch this ratio not for the numbers specifically but whether it is increasing or decreasing. That's really the key to ensuring your company isn't taking on too much debt.

A final note about the debt to equity ratio. It should definitely not be negative! If the ratio is negative it means that the net worth of the company is negative, that is, it has more liabilities than assets. If the company is seeking a bank loan, very few bankers will extend loans when a company has a negative net worth unless there are extenuating circumstances and there are assets that the company can pledge. A negative net worth means that the company is probably in trouble because it has been losing money for a long period of time.

The other debt ratio is long-term debt to equity (LTD/E) This financial ratio looks at how much long-term debt the company owes. Calculate this ratio by looking at the balance sheet. It is calculated:

Long-Term Liabilities / Total Equity

Again, make sure that items that should be in long-term liabilities are there. If there are bank loans and the current portion of these loans is included, then this ratio will be overstated.

In most cases, this ratio should be equal to or greater than zero and less than one. It should definitely not be negative! (See the explanation for debt to equity.)

The long-term debt to equity ratio looks at long-term liabilities divided by equity. It tells whether the company is burdened with huge amounts of long-term debts, which will be paid in many years. You want this amount of debt to be as low as possible.

If you have a decreasing long-term debt to equity (which is good), your company will either have increasing profitability or be paying off some of its long-term debts. If this ratio is increasing, this is a warning sign. The company has decreasing profitability and is incurring more debt.

71

Ignoring Receivable Days Trends

||||||||||||||||||||||||||||||||||||

"Crap. We have a collection problem."

This business owner totally ignored his receivable days trends. When he finally looked at it, he realized that the number of days was increasing, meaning that some of his customers were not paying their bills. Thankfully, he recognized the issue and resolved it before a cash crunch occurred.

Normal receivable days were around 45, and the number slowly inched up until it was 60 days. That meant paying expenses two months before getting paid. From that point, he hired internal collections employee. The receivable days dropped and stayed around 45 days.

The receivable days are calculated from the receivable turns ratio. The receivable days are the number of days between the time your company sends out an invoice and receives payment for that invoice.

These ratios measure how efficiently the company collects its receivables. The turns are calculated on annual sales. Calculate this ratio by using both the profit and loss statement and the balance sheet. It is calculated:

Annualized Sales / Trade Accounts Receivable

or

Anualized Sales / (Trade Accounts Receivable + Cash)

To annualize sales, take the year-to-date sales times 12 divided by the month of the fiscal year that you are in. For example, if year-to-date sales are $100,000 and the company is in month 5 of its fiscal year, multiply $100,000 times 12 and divide that by 5. Then divide that number by trade accounts receivable. Use only the trade accounts receivable—the amounts that customers owe the company. Do not include employee receivables or owner receivables.

If more than 50% of the revenues are COD revenues, then use accounts receivable plus cash as the divisor.

Now calculate receivable days.

Receivable days measures how efficiently the company collects its receivables. The days are calculated from the receivable turns figure. It is calculated:

365 / Receivable Turns

If receivable days are increasing, that means more billing, less COD sales, and less collections.

On the other hand, if the ratio is decreasing, there is less billing, more COD, or more collections activities. Try to maintain receivable days under 45 days. If the company has mainly COD revenues, receivable days should be under 30 days.

If receivable days continue to increase from month to month, you have a collection problem. Call the customers with overdue accounts and find out when you will be getting payment for the work you completed. Or, if you hire someone to handle collections, make sure you review your accounts receivable list every week and get progress reports on collection activities.

72

Not Checking Journal Entries

IIIIIIIIIIIIIIIIII|IIIIIIIIIIIIIIIIII

"Where did the cash go?"

A business owner had an employee who was responsible for accounts receivable. Her job included calling customers when receivables were not paid on time.

Every month the company owner printed out an aged receivables list and kept track of who owed the company money and how much of it was current and past due.

Unfortunately the company didn't always get their monthly financial statements in a timely manner. Many times the owner was looking at them three or more months later (January's financial statements were ready in April). So, he didn't have a good grasp on the accounts receivable balance on the statement because it was from a few months ago.

However, he did watch cash coming in the door. He did watch the accounts receivable balances and was told when large checks were received. Despite the checks coming in, cash was always tight. Sometimes the company just scraped by to make payroll. Other times they couldn't pay all of their vendors on time. This didn't make sense given the amount of cash that was coming in the door.

He couldn't figure out what was wrong.

Following my rules, he asked to see an aged receivables list. It looked right. Then he compared the accounts receivable on the aged receivables list to the receivables stated on the balance sheet. That was right too. Something just didn't add up.

He had to dig further. He reviewed the journal entries for the months. It was there! He saw cash withdrawals and entries to make accounts receivable on the balance sheet match the aged receivables report.

Since journal entries never appear on the financial statement, the owner never saw the changes.

When he dug deeper, he found that the accounts receivable clerk stole more than $100,000 over the time period she was there.

Always look at the journal entries with the financial statements. Make sure they are legitimate.

73

Not Saving Cash

||||||||||||||||||||||||||||||||||||||||

"I don't know where my next paycheck is coming from."

A salesperson said this. He was working for a company along the Gulf Coast that was hit when a hurricane devastated the area.

He was concerned. The business was hit hard and was not operating. How could he survive? How could the business survive?

Even business interruption insurance would take time to pay the business. The company needed cash.

You must have a savings account to rely on.

How much should be in it? The answer is another question: What is your risk-taking appetite?

Here's my formula for the amount of cash that should be in savings.

1. Estimate total payroll expenses for your busiest month and multiply by 3.
2. Estimate total overhead expenses in your busiest month. Multiply by 3 to 6, depending on your risk appetite.
3. Add the two amounts.

How do you build it? Save 1% of every dollar that comes in the door. If the company gets a check for $10,000, put $100 in that savings account. There still is $9,900 to use for operations. The 1% builds up quickly.

Another cash-building rainy day account is the recurring revenue savings account. When customers pay in advance, they are paying on a bet. Their money is not the company's money until the work is performed or the product is sent. Put it away! Then, once the work has been performed or the product sent, the cash is earned. However, don't take it out of the savings account unless it is needed for operations. Keep it there as long as possible. The goal is for the recurring revenue savings account value to be higher than the recurring revenue deferred income account value on the balance sheet.

Build your savings account. It could pay for the cleanup after a hurricane or another pandemic.

Not Reconciling Vendor and Credit Card Bills Each Month

|||||||||||||||||||||||||||||||||||||||||||

"I'm too busy to reconcile the gas bill."

A bookkeeper actually said this to me. I immediately reported what she said to the company owner. The gas bill got reconciled.

Your bookkeeper should never be too busy to reconcile every vendor and credit card account before paying the bill. With respect to gas and credit card bills, make sure that the employees are filling up your truck and not their personal vehicles. Make sure they are using company credit cards for company purchases only. If your bookkeeper notices an employee's fuel bill much higher than the others or personal charges on company credit cards, they must investigate.

Many companies require employees to report the mileage on their trucks when they get gas. The mileage is checked during a routine truck inspection to make sure it matches what the driver reported.

Your policy manual should clearly state what the company credit cards are to be used for and what they are not to be used for. If your bookkeeper sees drinks, food, and other items purchased in a gas station or other places on company credit cards, then these expenses must be repaid.

It's never too busy to check receipts!

Not Reconciling Bank Statements Each Month

||||||||||||||||||||||||||||||||||||||

If you can't trust a nun, who can you trust?

In December 2017, two California nuns were caught embezzling $500,000 from the education and tuition fund of the St. James Catholic Church in Torrance, California. They used the money to gamble in Las Vegas!

They were convicted in 2022.

Two significant details:

1. It took a change in leadership to find it, because the school had always operated in the black and no one suspected anything.
2. The nuns discovered a "forgotten bank account" that was set up by the school in 1997 and used it to deposit some of the tuition money.

So, if nuns, who are supposed to be trustworthy and beyond reproach, can steal, anyone can steal, including a family member.

You, as the business owner, are responsible for every dollar that comes in to and goes out of your business. Look at all of your bank accounts every day, review financial statements every month, and watch the checks that you sign.

This takes a trip to the bank to make sure there isn't an account that was opened in 1997 that has a little money going in and out. If these amounts are so little compared to your daily cash inflow and outgo, you probably won't notice it if you've forgotten about an account. However, $25 per week is $1,300 per year...for how many years?

Each of your bank accounts should be reconciled every month. You should request and review the printouts of the reconciliations. If your bookkeeper does them and doesn't show the reports, they could fake the reconciliations or not do them. This is another easy way to steal.

|||||||||||||||||||||||||||||||||||||||

DUMB MISTAKES:

Profit and Loss Statements

|||||||||||||||||||||||||||||||||||||||

Your profit and loss statement (P&L), also called an income statement, is your monthly and sometimes daily scorecard. It tells you whether revenues are greater than expenses and you have a profit. It tells you whether expenses are greater than profits and you have a loss.

76

Thinking That Your P&L Tells You If Your Company Is Profitable

||||||||||||||||||||||||||||||||||||

"I get month-to-date and year-to-date values every month. I see where I am going."

This business owner had a false sense of security. He didn't look at what was really going on with the company. Even though his P&L said he had a profitable month, his current ratio trend showed a different picture. It was declining even though the company showed a profit, there was less profit each month only a little bit so he never dug in.

If you are on a cash basis for accounting (see Mistake 5), you'll never know if your company is profitable.

Assuming you are on an accrual basis, the monthly profit and loss statement tells you that your company is profitable or has a loss for that month. It does not tell you if your company is profitable for the long term—that is, profitability. A one-month profit is good for that month. However, how about over three months? A year?

That's where profitability tells you that your company is headed in the right direction. True profitability is shown on your balance sheet. Your current ratio (see Mistake 68) shows your company profitability. Generally, an increasing current ratio means increasing profitability.

Profit and loss statements show short-term profit or loss. They start over each month or year.

They do not show if profits were a little higher or lower than the month before. Profits are essential. However, are they trending higher or lower? Your company's current ratio answers this question.

Balance sheets are continuous. They show you increasing or decreasing profitability over a long period of time.

Not Realizing That Your P&L Starts Over Each Month

||||||||||||||||||||||||||||||||||||

"Thank goodness 2020 is over."

Many people not only business owners were thrilled that the year 2020 was over. Everyone looked forward to a better 2021 and hopefully less COVID-19.

Profit and loss statements start over too. For companies whose year end is December, January 1 starts at zero revenue and zero expense.

Your company had a profitable January. Great. Start over on February 1. The goal is to be profitable again in February. Every month you start over.

Your company had a loss in January. Find out why and learn from it. Your company has another chance to be profitable in February.

Profit and loss statements start over every month and every year. If the company showed a really profitable month, great. If it had a really bad month from a profit perspective, the first of the next month starts over. Just make sure that month is profitable. Too many unprofitable months can be a recipe for disaster.

Counting Non-Operational Revenues and Expenses as Operational Revenues and Expenses

IIIIIIIIIIIIIIIIII|IIIIIIIIIIIIIIIII

"We made more money this year than we ever made."

A business owner said this. Looking at his P&L, he counted the forgiveness of the PPP loan as part of operational profit. It wasn't. That forgiveness had nothing to do with operational profit. Yes, forgiveness of loans is considered income; however, that is other income, not income from operations.

Your profit and loss statement should divide operations income and expenses from non-operations income and expenses. Your statements should have net operating profit income and then list other income and other expenses. Once other income and other expenses are taken into account, the bottom line net profit before taxes is shown in Figure 7.

      Revenues
− Cost of Goods Sold
= Gross Profit
− Overhead
= Net Operating Profit
+ Other Income
− Other Expenses
= Net Profit before Taxes
− Taxes
= Net Profit

Figure 7. Profit and loss statement format

Here are examples of other income:

- Interest received from savings accounts and other company investments.
- Forgiveness of loans, such as the PPP loans that were given during the COVID-19 pandemic.
- Sales of assets that have been fully depreciated on your balance sheet (for example, if the company sold a truck for $1,000 and it had zero value on the balance sheet, that $1,000 is other income).

Here are examples of other expenses:

- Legal or other expenses incurred that are not related to day to day operations (that is, purchase of another business).
- Bad debt write-offs where the bad debt didn't occur in the operational year (that is, you had accounts receivable on the balance sheet for work that was done two years prior to the year it was written off).
- Sales of assets that where the sale price is less than the amount shown on your balance sheet (that is, if your company sold a truck for $1,000 and its value on the balance sheet is $2,000, that is a $1,000 other loss).

If you include these non-operational income and expenses in operations, you'll never know if your operations are profitable.

79

Recognizing Sales as Revenue

||||||||||||||||||||||||||||||||||||||

The two terms are different but unfortunately are used interchangeably. If you report sales instead of revenue on your profit and loss statement, it might be wrong.

Here's why: a sale is a sale. Revenue is that portion of the sale that is billed and accounted for. If your company collects COD for sales, then revenue equals sales each month. Here are two examples where sales and revenues are not equal.

Example 1: Project that takes 4 months to complete

You sell a $1 million project, which is to be completed over a four-month period. The sale is $1 million. The entire $1 million does not appear on your profit and loss statement the month that it is sold unless the entire project is completed in a month. If the entire job is completed in a month, sales and revenues are the same.

If the project is performed over a period of months, generally the project is billed over several months.

The revenue, which appears on your profit and loss statement, is the amount that is billed for that month. The total revenues over the period of time that the project is completed equal the sale amount. If the project takes four months from start to finish, and a quarter of the project is completed each month, then the revenues that are accounted for on your profit and loss statements are $250,000 a month, not $1 million. The expenses incurred to produce those revenues are also in the same month.

Example 2: Recurring revenue program paid in advance (or on monthly billing)

Assume your customer pays you $250 each January for their recurring revenue program. The program activities are performed in April and October.

The sale is $250. It is recorded as $250 deferred income on your balance sheet rather than a $250 sale on your profit and loss statement.

Why? You received money for work you have not performed. This is a liability to perform work.

When you do the first activity in April, your liability to perform is cut in half; $125 is now recognized as revenues on your P&L and your deferred income is cut in half.

You must recognize the revenue in the month you performed the activities. If you don't, the company will be busy doing work and have nothing to show for it on your P&L. This is why I often hear the complaint "We're busy and losing money." If the recurring revenue program is priced and accounted for properly, you'll be busy and at least breaking even, because the revenue and expense are accounted for properly.

Thinking That Gross Profit Is Net Profit

||||||||||||||||||||||||||||||||||||

"We made a 40% profit last month."

This statement was made by a manager to his team members during a meeting. The team walked out of the meeting thinking that the company was doing incredibly well and that they should all get raises!

I explained to the manager that he told the team the wrong profit percentage. He gave them the gross profit percentage rather than the net profit percentage. The number he gave to the team didn't include overhead expenses!

During the next meeting he explained his mistake. He mentioned that if the department really had a 40% net profit, then everyone would get huge bonuses. Unfortunately, the department's net profit percentage was much lower: 10%. The last month he had not included the overhead costs like rent, utility bills, and other expenses to keep the doors open. The team understood.

Gross profit is revenue less the direct costs to produce those revenues. Gross margin, the percentage of gross profit, is gross profit divided by sales. Gross profit is always a dollar value. Gross margin in always a percentage. Net profit is gross profit less overhead expenses. Net profit percentage is net profit divided by sales. Net profit is always a dollar value.

Make sure you report the correct percentage to the employees and they understand that gross profit is not net profit.

81

Having a Negative Gross Margin on Your P&L

||||||||||||||||||||||||||||||||||||||

"This can't be right."

"Why?"

"The statement shows a negative gross margin. What did you miss?"

This is the conversation that a company owner had with his book-keeper.

The owner discovered that the bookkeeper was lazy. She closed the months without all of the revenue that should be in that month. She had not completed all the billing for work that had been performed that month. She did enter all of the expenses for that month. She said that she was "too busy" to bill (see Mistake 9)!

Since all of the expenses but not all of the revenues were in that month, the gross margin was negative. This means that if the company buys a part for $1, it sells for less than $1.

The owner knew the pricing was right. This was simply the case of a lazy bookkeeper.

Gross margins cannot be negative except in warranty situations. No business owner will knowingly buy a part and sell it for less than he bought it for. In warranty situations, you have cost without revenue since you doing work to repair or fix something that was not done right the first time. In these cases you have zero revenue and direct cost, so your gross profit and gross margin will be negative.

Ignoring Changes in Gross Margins

||||||||||||||||||||||||||||||||||||||

Assuming your pricing is consistent, your gross margins should be consistent. If it is supposed to be 42%, it should be 42% all the time. It should not be 42% one month and 45% the next. Nor should it be 42% one month and 38% the next month.

If your company's profit and loss statement reports changing gross margins, find out why these changes are happening.

Places to look:

- People are taking longer on projects than was budgeted for that project.
- Materials used are more than were estimated.
- Additional costs incurred that were not estimated for the project.
- Financial statement fruit salad (see Mistake 86).

If it was a mistake in a proposal or estimate, what did you learn so that you don't do it again?

If it was higher material prices, you must increase your proposal prices (see Mistake 50).

All companies who sell products know they have cost of sales and gross margin. If your company is a service company and does not sell physical products, you still have a cost of sales—the people who provide your services. You still have a gross margin.

A consistent gross margin means that your gross margin varies by less than 2% around the desired gross margin.

For example, your company's gross margin in supposed to be 53% and it is actually like this:

Month	Gross Margin
1	53%
2	51%
3	49%
4	55%
5	56%
6	48%

This is not a consistent gross margin. A margin changing from 49% to 55% in one month (months 3 and 4) is too large of a change. You need to find out why the change was so great. Were all the revenues and costs incurred producing those revenues accounted for in the same month?

Here's what gross margins should look like:

Month	Gross Margin
1	53%
2	52%
3	51%
4	52%
5	54%
6	53%

This is a consistent gross margin range. The gross margin is varying only by 1% to 2% around the desired gross margin of 53%.

Make sure your company's gross margins are consistent around the value it should be based on pricing.

Not Tracking Materials Taken for a Job against Materials Estimated for a Job

‖‖‖‖‖‖‖‖‖‖‖‖‖‖‖‖‖‖‖‖‖‖‖‖‖‖‖‖

"I'm happy to help you build your service department. First, we have to fix the hole in your warehouse."

"What do you mean?"

"Materials are walking out of the warehouse, and no one knows what they are taking."

This was a conversation between a business owner and me. According to my calculations, about $500,000 was lost in materials.

The warehouse procedures changed immediately. Material lists for projects appeared. Only one person could get the inventory ready for the jobs. He completed the material list requirements and put those materials in a specific place in the warehouse.

Any extra materials that were not used were brought back to the warehouse, and the amount of that material was deducted from the job expenses.

Warehouse and truck inventory was accurately counted. This was painful, and it took a few weeks to get it accomplished. A procedure for monthly counting was put in place during the initial inventory count.

Warehouse inventory was then counted monthly and matched against the balance sheet. When the numbers got close, the count was moved to quarterly and then annually. The company never had that amount of inventory loss again.

You must know what materials are coming into the warehouse and what materials are going out for jobs so that job costing can be accurate (see Mistake 88).

84

Thinking That All Payroll Expenses
Are Company Expenses

|||||||||||||||||||||||||||||||||||||||||

"Payroll expense is double what it should be."

This was my analysis, based on the payroll reports filed with the federal and state revenue departments.

The company was taking the entire payroll expense as an overhead expense.

This is wrong. Here's why.

There are two types of payroll expenses—employee payroll expenses and company payroll expenses. For those businesses, mainly lifestyle businesses, where there is a sole proprietor or a one-person LLC, the sole proprietor bears the employee and the employer payroll expenses.

Employees get payroll taxes and withholding taxes taken from their paychecks. Employers match the employee payroll taxes. They do not have to match the withholding taxes. The employer match is an overhead expense along with unemployment and other payroll taxes that the employee doesn't have to pay.

Make sure that you don't expense the employee's portion of payroll expenses. It makes your net operating profit lower than it should be. (See Mistake 65 for proper accounting for payroll expenses).

Counting Overhead Expenses in Direct Costs or Direct Costs in Overhead

‖‖‖‖‖‖‖‖‖‖‖‖‖‖‖‖‖‖‖‖‖‖‖‖‖

"Our gross margin is excellent. I'm pleased."

"You shouldn't be."

"What do you mean?"

"All of your labor is in overhead."

"So?"

"Your gross margin is much higher than it should be."

The profit and loss statement showed the labor to produce the products was not in cost of goods sold. All the labor was accounted for in overhead. Labor to produce products is a direct cost. By not putting production labor where it belonged, the company financial statements showed an artificially high gross margin.

Direct costs (that is, costs of goods sold) are those costs that you incur because you generated revenue. Often I see overhead costs in direct costs and direct costs in overhead costs.

Here are examples of overhead costs in direct costs:

- Payroll for an office employee
- A normal direct cost, such as vacation, holiday, sick, meeting, training, or any other time that is paid but isn't used to generate revenue.
- Payroll for a manager who doesn't generate revenues

Here are examples of direct costs in overhead:

- Sales commissions.

- Credit card charges for revenues paid for by credit cards.
- All hourly and salary expenses. Direct cost labor should be in direct costs.

Make sure that all direct costs are in cost of goods sold and all overhead costs are in overhead. Then you have a better chance of ensuring your gross margins are consistent (see Mistake 81).

Counting Inventory as Cost of Goods Sold

IIIIIIIIIIIIIIII|IIIIIIIIIIIIIIII

"Our P&L showed a loss this month. No way. We price correctly and we were busy."

Upon examination of the profit and loss statement, materials expense was much higher than it should have been. The inventory was expensed on the profit and loss statement rather than added to inventory on the balance sheet, where it belongs.

If your company purchased a lot of inventory because your supplier "had a great deal," you could have lost money that month if that "great deal" was counted as a materials expense rather than inventory. (I see this on financial statements were the cost of goods sold includes a purchases category rather than a materials expense category.)

In this case, in the months the company purchased materials for use later, the net operating profit will be lower than it should be. In the months it used that material, the net operating profit will be higher than it should be. Neither is correct.

If you purchase materials for a job, that expense goes into cost of goods sold. It is not inventory.

If you purchase materials because you think you will need them for a job, that is inventory.

If you don't track inventory and all material purchases go into cost of goods sold, your gross margins and your net profit will be lower than they actually are. This doesn't really matter much for lifestyle businesses. It matters a lot for tool and transformation businesses. Inventory is a bet (see Mistake 57).

Having Financial Statement Fruit Salad

|||||||||||||||||||||||||||||||||||||||

"We're really busy, but our P&L shows a loss. I don't get it."

This statement was made to me by a company owner who didn't realize that he had financial statement "fruit salad." He was really busy. He had just accounted for the work he was doing in previous months. He had financial statement fruit salad.

Financial statement fruit salad is when a profit and loss statement reports revenues with no expenses incurred producing the work for revenues, or expenses are reported in a month without the revenues generated by those expenses.

For example, if revenues (apple month) are put in one month and the expenses incurred to produce those revenues are put in another month (orange month), you have fruit salad (apples and oranges) when you look at your profit and loss statement and job cost.

Financial statement fruit salad is disastrous. You want only apple salad (or orange salad, peach salad, or another fruit of your choice). Revenues must match expenses in the same month. This helps ensure that you can make accurate decisions about your revenues and direct costs. Never report sales on your profit and loss statement without the work to produce that sale in the single month.

If you put revenues in one month and expenses in another month, you are fooling yourself.

Here's what happens: the month with the revenues and no expenses will look like a great month from a profit perspective. You'll probably be feeling great about the business. The month that has the expenses and no revenues will be a profit loser, and you may feel bad about the business. Neither is accurate. You can't make good business decisions with inaccurate financial statements.

Seasonality can mask your opinion of your financial statements. Many times the thought is, *We didn't do enough work, so we should expect a loss this month.* Even in slow months (from a revenue perspective) your gross margin still should be consistent. There may not be enough revenue volume to cover the overhead, so the financial statements show a loss.

With enough recurring revenue, accounted for properly, your company should at least break even in slower months.

Make sure you don't have fruit salad in your financial statements.

88

Reporting No Rent or Double Rent on a Monthly P&L Statement

||||||||||||||||||||||||||||||||||||||||

Most businesses have a rent expense every month. There are utility expenses every month. There is a telephone expense every month.

You know these expenses should be fairly consistent and be reported each month.

If they are not there or they appear to be double what they should be, then your bookkeeper forgot to put the monthly expense in the month it should be in and added it to a different month.

Your net operating profit will be wrong. It will be too high where these expenses are missing and too low when double expenses are reported.

Make sure all expenses are in the month they were incurred so that your financial statements will be accurate and you can make good business decisions based on what they are reporting.

89

Not Job Costing

||||||||||||||||||||||||||||||||||

"I'm happy. My job cost says that we've achieved a 35% gross margin on our latest project."

Is this a reason to be happy? Maybe and maybe not. Gross margin doesn't tell the whole story.

I've known companies to achieve a 35% gross margin on a project and still lose money on that project. Unfortunately, this happens frequently. Here's why.

Job costing is a profit and loss statement for the work performed. The net profit per hour (see Mistake 43) is the critical bottom line.

Job costing should start with the revenue generated, the number of billable hours on the job, the total direct cost, and the total overhead cost. Overhead is the number of hours times the overhead cost per hour (see Mistake 42).

The net profit is determined and then divided by the number of job hours. Taking overhead into consideration is the only job costing that counts. (Some companies erroneously stop at the gross profit and gross margin line.) Overhead must be taken into consideration!

There should also be a space to list the team members who worked on that job. You might find that some team members have a higher net profit per hour than other team members. Knowing which teams are most productive gives you the knowledge of which crews need training.

Relying only on gross margins to determine whether a job went well or not is dangerous. You have to know and understand what your net profit per hour and overhead cost per hour are. The only thing that really counts is the net profit per hour that you are generating, which is calculated through job costing. That's what you can convert to cash and take to the bank.

Relying on data that stops at gross margin or gross profit doesn't tell the whole story.

Not Looking at Labor Productivity Ratio Trends

||||||||||||||||||||||||||||||||||||||

How productive are your employees?

Your labor productivity ratio (also called compensation percentage ratio) trend tells you the answer.

Labor productivity or compensation ratio answers the question, "For every revenue dollar, how much is spent on payroll and payroll taxes?"

The ratio is:

Total Payroll + Payroll Taxes / Revenue

To determine your company's productivity ratio, divide total payroll plus payroll taxes by total sales each month. Payroll includes all compensation, which is the same as the gross wages number you report to the IRS on Form 941 each month. If owner compensation is accounted for differently than on Form 941, then add the owner compensation to the Form 941 gross wages for the month. Payroll taxes include FICA, Medicare, state unemployment, and federal unemployment. Do not include worker's compensation, health insurance, or other benefits.

Track this number each month. It may go up and down, depending on seasonality. This is your baseline number.

To increase productivity, decrease your compensation percentage ratio (you are spending less on payroll and payroll taxes with a decreasing ratio). Here are some suggestions:

- Post the compensation ratio each month. If you have different departments, calculate and post the ratio for each department. What gets watched gets improved.
- Make it fun: have a contest around decreasing the compensation ratio. For example, if your compensation ratio is 45% and you want to lower it to 35%, have a contest with a great prize when it gets to and stays at or below 35%. This 10% decrease in payroll and payroll taxes for the same sales volume goes directly to your bottom line. You can share in the savings with the people who helped get it there.
- Increasing sales with the same level of payroll decreases the compensation ratio. Your employees might come up with a way to increase sales with the same number of working hours per month. Again, this savings falls to your bottom line.
- Do not estimate projects in two-hour increments. For example, a six-hour project will magically get stretched to eight hours. A two-hour project magically takes until lunch. Estimate project in four-hour increments: 4, 8, 12, 16, 20, 24 hours, and so on.
- Monitor overtime hours. If someone is spending an hour on social media or personal phone calls and then receiving an hour of overtime per week, cut out the overtime. There is enough time during the day to get the job done, assuming social media and personal phone calls are eliminated. Also, make sure that if you issue company-owned phones. Then you can monitor calls.

Make sure your labor productivity ratio is decreasing or constant.

Ignoring Your Profit and Loss Trends

||||||||||||||||||||||||||||||||||||

Looking at graphs rather than numbers (I give specific examples in my book *The Courage to Be Profitable*) shows the company's profit and loss trends.

Graph revenue, gross profit, total overhead, and net operating profit. Make sure that the data in each category are accurate (see Mistake 84).

Graph your profit and loss data in two ways: monthly data and trailing data.

Monthly Data

The monthly data graphs of your ratios take the values directly from the month calculations. Each month in the spreadsheet is the exact data that is reported on your balance sheet and profit and loss statement.

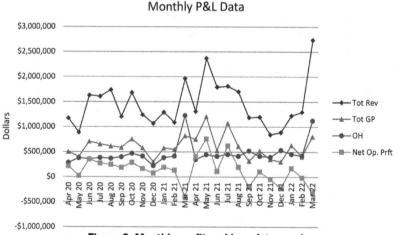

Figure 8. Monthly profit and loss data graph

Trailing Data

Trailing data graphs look at a year's worth of data a month at a time. They are generated by adding 12 months of data and dividing it by 12 to get the month's data point. For example, the revenue point for January 2022 would be adding the revenues from February 2021 through January 2022 and dividing this result by 12. You could do trailing data by week (and divide by 52) or even by quarter. However, for the purposes of this financial product, analyzing data on a monthly basis is sufficient, so trailing data is calculated on a monthly basis.

Trailing data needs at least 14 months of data. With less than 14 months of data, you cannot create an accurate trailing data graph.

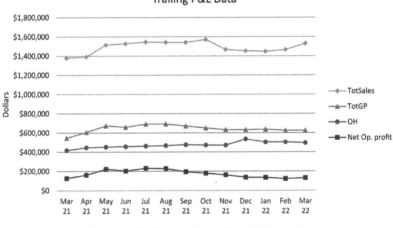

Figure 9. Trailing profit and loss data graph

Your trailing graphs show you whether revenues are increasing, remaining flat, or decreasing. If they are decreasing, you need to find out why and take action before the lack of revenues causes the lack of profits.

Your trailing graphs show you whether gross profit is increasing, remaining flat, or decreasing. The gross profit line should be parallel to the revenue line. If it is not, then you are selling more at a lower profit.

Your trailing graphs show you whether overhead is increasing, remaining flat, or decreasing. It should remain flat or decrease. If it is increasing, what additional overhead expenses are you incurring? Do you need them?

Your trailing graphs show you whether net operating profit is increasing, remaining flat, or decreasing. If it is decreasing, and the data is accurate, what can you do to turn the decreasing profits around?

Figures 8 and 9 show the monthly and trailing data for a stable company. Its profits are fairly consistent, and the company is growing at a pace to match increasing costs. Profitability is decreasing slightly, so actions need to be taken to stabilize or increase profitability (two things to check are making sure prices are increasing with costs and making sure labor productivity is increasing).

Track trailing data. It shows you the profit and loss trends for your company. If the trends are going the wrong way, determine what is wrong and fix the issues.

||||||||||||||||||||||||||||||||||

DUMB MISTAKES:

Theft

||||||||||||||||||||||||||||||||||

As a business owner, you are a target for theft. Not only can your bookkeeper steal from you, but your other employees, your suppliers, and others in foreign countries can steal, too. My book *The Ugly Truth about Cash* reveals 50 ways people can steal from you and what to do about it. I promised at the end of the book I would reveal more ingenious and creative ways people stole. They are described in the mistakes on the next few pages.

92

Trusting Your Bookkeeper

||||||||||||||||||||||||||||||||||||

"I never thought this would happen to me. I trust my bookkeeper."

The goal of a good embezzler is to become a trusted bookkeeper.

I got an email from a business owner who had taken my Building Profit and Wealth class. He said that he was having problems with his bookkeeper and asked whether I would help him.

Of course.

We set a time to talk.

Background: On the second day of the Building Profit and Wealth class, I go over the procedures you need to put in place to keep the honest people honest.

When we talked, I discovered that this owner had hired a bookkeeper when the company was in trouble financially. She came in and cleaned up the books. The owner could tell where the company was financially so he could make the decisions necessary to get the company profitable again.

The bookkeeper was instrumental in getting clean financials. She befriended the owner's wife. He stopped looking at financial statements every month because he trusted her.

The embezzler had become the trusted bookkeeper.

The owner made a decision to go to direct deposit for their weekly payroll. This was the opportunity the patient embezzler was looking for.

She would take a direct deposit check and then she would write an additional check to herself, cash it, and delete the check from Quick-Books. Since she was responsible for the reconciliations (and they were *never* checked to make sure they were right), the owner couldn't see the deleted check.

The owner finally paid attention when he couldn't understand why he was starting to have cash flow problems.

When he called me with this situation, his comment was, "I sat in your class thinking that this would never happen to me...and it did."

She embezzled about $60,000 before she was caught. At a 10% net profit, this owner has to generate $600,000 in revenue to pay for this mistake. Ouch!

Giving Your Bookkeeper Check-Signing Authority

||||||||||||||||||||||||||||||||||||||

Bookkeepers should never have check-signing authority. If they write a check to themself, then it is within the bounds of acceptability, because you gave them the ability to sign checks. That means the bookkeeper can sign any check, even one written to themself!

It is much harder to prosecute someone with check-signing authority for writing a check to themself. If they don't have check-signing authority, it is a criminal offense. If they have check-signing authority, and they embezzle, you are partially at fault because you gave that person the ability to write checks to anyone. It is a civil rather than a criminal case.

Bookkeepers should not want check-signing authority either.

Why? If the payroll taxes are not paid, the IRS can request payment of those taxes from anyone who has check-signing authority, even people who are not owners or managers of the company. This means your bookkeeper, your wife, your mother, or your children are at risk if they have check-signing authority.

Bookkeepers prepare checks for owner's signature. The owner then signs all checks. Watch what you sign, and question anything that looks unusual.

Not Looking at Your Bank Accounts Every Day

IIIIIIIIIIIIIIIIII|IIIIIIIIIIIIIIIII

Your employees can steal from you. Outsiders can steal from you too.

It doesn't matter where you are; you can log in to all of your bank accounts every day. It takes less than five minutes to do this. Look at the checks, automatic withdrawals, and deposits. Make sure they make sense.

A client's bookkeeper did this (the owner did not) and noticed two deposits for less than $1.00. He thought the owner was setting up a new account and didn't question him. The next day the bank called asking whether the owner had authorized a $50,000 withdrawal! Obviously the answer was no. The account was shut down. Those two little deposits were making sure the account was valid.

Tool and transformation businesses should have at minimum an operations bank account, a payroll account, and a savings account to put your recurring revenue deposits and 1% of revenues in weekly.

Look at all of your bank accounts—both checking and savings. Make sure everything looked valid.

Signing Checks without Looking at What You Are Signing

||||||||||||||||||||||||||||||||||||||||

I was sitting in an owner's office discussing some observations I had made. He was half listening because he was signing payroll checks.

All of a sudden he started laughing. I promise you, what we were talking about was not funny.

"What's going on?" I asked.

He handed me a payroll check that should have been for a little over $1,000 but was written for a little over $10,000! The bookkeeper had made a mistake when calculating payroll and printing payroll checks.

Can you imagine what would have happened had he not looked at what he was signing? The employee would have received the extra $9,000, rushed to the bank, cashed the check, and went on a spending spree. Thanks, boss, for the bonus!

Getting that $9,000 back would have been difficult and taken months or even years through payroll deduction.

Always look at what you are signing. For vendor payments, make sure the check matches the purchase order (if there is one) and the invoice. If something doesn't look right, don't sign the check until you get backup information to make sure the check is correct.

What if payments are made through ACH, credit card or vendor portals, or other online payment methods, such as PayPal?

Those payments still should have backup documentation proving that the payments are correct. Look at the backup. Look at your bank accounts daily (see Mistake 93).

Having a Signature Stamp

||||||||||||||||||||||||||||||||||||||

Many owners think that requiring two signatures on a check prevents theft. It doesn't if one of those signatures can be a signature stamp.

In the 40+ years I have been consulting with business owners, one of the most difficult things I've ever had to do was tell two partners that a third partner was stealing at least $50,000 a year from their business.

It probably was more. However, I felt horrible. I didn't want to dig any further.

How did it happen?

Two signatures were required on all checks. One of the partners had his signature on a stamp, which the bookkeeper partner used along with his own signature. He wrote checks to himself and coded them to penalties, interest, and other accounts. The other partners never reviewed the financial statements. After all, they trusted their partner who did the books. As a result, they didn't question the penalties even though their payroll taxes were always paid on time (so entries in this category didn't make sense). No one caught him until I investigated.

But what if you're going to be gone for a vacation and the bookkeeper says they need a signature stamp?

This happened with one of my clients, who had a signature stamp that only he used when, in the past, checks needed to be signed when he was out of town.

The bookkeeper insisted that she needed the signature stamp since the owner was going on vacation. I said it was ridiculous. Bills could be paid before the owner left or after he returned.

She said that the owner didn't trust her and she absolutely needed that stamp. He explained that trust is not the issue. He didn't want any checks signed by anyone else. (I had explained the dangers of a bookkeeper having a signature stamp.)

Since the owner had not destroyed the stamp yet (he eventually did), I told him to put it somewhere in his home where his daughter could find it. If the bookkeeper absolutely needed to write a check, then she could explain why to his daughter and get her approval, and he would tell the daughter where to find the stamp. She could get it, bring it to the bookkeeper, stamp the check, and bring the stamp back to his home.

Since payroll was through direct deposit, unless there was an emergency, no checks needed to be written for payroll while he was gone.

The owner left on vacation. The hidden signature stamp was never needed while he was gone.

Not Checking Vendor Lists Once a Quarter

||||||||||||||||||||||||||||||||||||||

It's very easy to set up a business account with a similar name to a legitimate vendor. For example, your real vendor may be ABC Corporation. An embezzler could set up a checking account with ABC Company or ABC as the name on the account.

When you are signing checks, you may not notice a second name that is similar to that of your legitimate vendor, especially if there are purchase orders and invoices behind them to verify the amount of the check. Embezzlers are patient and creative. They can easily create purchase orders and invoices that look legitimate.

The best defense you have is printing and carefully reviewing your vendor list once a quarter. The owner should be the one to print the list. Make sure you ask for active and inactive vendors when you print the list.

Review the list. If there are two or more similar-sounding names, find out why. Make sure any incorrect or illegitimate vendor names are deleted.

In addition, bookkeepers should never be able to add vendors. This is a permission setting in your accounting software. Why? Because the embezzler can create a vendor for a company that is the embezzler's company with a similar name to one of your real vendors.

Not Tracking Electronic Payments

||||||||||||||||||||||||||||||||||||||

A business owner was looking at the aged receivables report and noticed several service customers who, according to the report, hadn't paid for the service at their homes. This was strange, because the company's service policy was COD and the technicians were supposed to collect at the end of each service call.

The company owner called the customers who were listed on the receivables report. He first made sure that the service was performed properly and the customers' systems were keeping their homes cool. He then asked, "Did you pay the technician at the end of the visit?"

Please notice he did not ask, "Why didn't you pay for the service?"

Every customer he called said yes, she paid the technician.

He then asked how they had paid. All said by credit card. He explained that the company didn't have a copy of the receipt. He asked if she would be willing to send the receipt to him.

All of the customers sent their receipts.

When he looked at the receipts, he noticed they all had his company's name on it. What he also saw was that the credit card was not being processed by his normal credit card company.

He continued the investigation and found that one technician had performed all of these service calls.

What had the technician done?

He applied for and got approved for a Square credit card processing account in the company's name, with the company's federal ID number and his bank account. (It's easy to get your company's federal ID number. Your company federal ID number is on the W-2 forms you give employees at the end of the year.)

When the customer paid by credit card, the technician swiped the card in the field using his own rather than the company's swipe device. The receipt had the company's name on it, so a customer would never think something was wrong.

The owner called the police, who investigated and arrested the technician. The technician was charged with seven federal crimes, including money laundering, ID theft, and more.

The amount the technician stole? Around $4,000. Imagine being in jail for a $4,000 theft.

I'm not saying that $4,000 is insignificant. What would have happened if this technician had stolen for months rather than weeks? The theft could have been tens of thousands of dollars more.

The company owner was thankful that he reviewed the weekly cash flow reports and the aged receivable and payable reports each week. He caught the thief quickly, before a lot of cash was stolen.

Always check your electronic payments.

99

Allowing the Same Person Who Creates
the Deposits to Go to the Bank

||||||||||||||||||||||||||||||||||||

"The bank just made a deposit error."

In one client's company, the receptionist opened the mail and took out the checks. She gave them to an accounts receivable team member, who added them to the cash received and created the deposit. The bookkeeper took the deposit to the bank.

The owner of the company happened to look at the deposit slip and the amount of the deposit on their bank statement. They differed by $10. The bookkeeper said that the bank had simply made a deposit error, and she would take care of it.

The owner trusted his bookkeeper and didn't think anything was wrong. However, he decided to call the bank himself and find out about the deposit. The banker told him that yes, the deposit was for $10 less than on the deposit slip. Then he started investigating. The deposits were often $10 to $20 less than the deposit slip said. Someone was stealing.

The only way he discovered the theft was that he had two different people involved. If the bookkeeper made the deposit and went to the bank, she could have easily made the deposit for $10 to $20 less and pocketed the cash.

In lifestyle and tool businesses, the owners should go to the bank. They don't have to prepare the deposits, but they should, as a rule, take them to the bank.

In transformation companies, there are generally many people involved with the financial side of the business. Owners should check the bank statements and insist on a reconciliation of cash and vendor accounts. They should match what is reported on the monthly financial statements.

Ignoring the Internal Revenue Service Theft Reporting Form

||||||||||||||||||||||||||||||||||||||

When you catch an embezzler, report the theft to the Internal Revenue Service. Many owners think they should report the theft on a 1099 or W-2 form. The best place to report it is on Form 3949A (as of the publication date of this book). This is an information referral form for reporting potential violations of the IRS law.

This way, the IRS will potentially start an investigation and an audit. At least the thief, if you don't prosecute, has the potential of going through a tax audit.

Check with your accountant for the latest tax rulings. As of now, embezzled funds are deductible in the year they are discovered. They are considered other expenses. Even if the theft has been happening for many years, the deduction is taken the year that they are discovered.

The tricky part is when you accept a repayment plan. These are taxable in subsequent years. If you charge interest, the repayment plan could be treated as a loan with interest. In these cases the repayment would be considered a reduction of debt with the interest expense reported as income.

Not Putting the Thieves in Jail

||||||||||||||||||||||||||||||||||||||

You've been unlucky enough to find that an employee has been stealing from you. Do you prosecute that person?

If you face this situation, you must first ask yourself if it is a civil or criminal matter. An example of a civil matter is when you give your bookkeeper check-signing authority and they steal. A criminal matter is when your bookkeeper forges a check or has direct withdrawals taken from your bank account without being an authorized signatory on that account. As a rule, it is easier to get a conviction in criminal matters.

What if the thief offers to repay the funds? For example, they could have a rich relative willing to repay the funds to keep them out of jail. Do you do it or not?

There is no right or wrong answer to this question. It depends on how much hassle you are willing to put up with during the investigation and court cases. Some owners learn from the event, put the proper procedures in place, and go on. They don't want the hassles of lawyers and courts. And they don't want the possibility of encountering a lenient judge who gives no jail time to a first-time offender.

Others feel that the thief should be prosecuted, no matter what. They put up with a few years of hassles for the satisfaction of seeing the thief in an orange jumpsuit.

Remember, if all you do is fire the thief, that person will steal from the next business owner he works for.

IMPLEMENT, PLEASE!

If you've never looked at your company's financial statements, especially a balance sheet, hopefully this book gives you the reasons to get and review your financial statements every month. Someone should be preparing them for you. Your job as owner is to do what you do best, whether it is sales or operations, and review the statements your accounting department prepares. Hire a bookkeeper to do the day-to-day entries and prepare the reports described in this book. You then review the reports.

If you found some mistakes that you are making with your business financials, please implement the corrections. Reading this book and doing nothing with what you've learned is a waste of your time.

Getting accurate, timely weekly cash flow reports and financial statements is not enough. You have to review them to discover any minor issues and resolve them before they become major crises. Implementation of what you find is the key to getting and staying profitable and building wealth.

Once you've built wealth, consider giving back to employees who've helped you along the way and to charitable organizations that you have a passion for. Sharing the wealth is key to success in the long term.

I wish you achievement of the goals you desire and a healthy business to support them.

YOUR BUSINESS FINANCIAL
HEALTH CHECKUP

Would you prefer to find out you have cancer when it is at stage 1 or stage 4?

The answer is Stage 1, of course—that's why you get regular health checkups.

Would you prefer to find out you are headed for a business problem before you are in the middle of a crisis?

Of course—that's why you get a business financial health checkup.

So, What Is a Business Financial Health Checkup?

Just like your body's vital signs are checked during a physical exam, you look at the financial vital signs of your business as reported each month on your profit and loss statement and balance sheet.

You see the trends so you can spot minor issues and take action before they become major problems.

Our team can help you implement what you discovered in *101 Dumb Financial Mistakes Business Owners Make and How to Avoid Them.*

How Does It Work?

1. Enter your financial statements each month.
2. We analyze your statements and produce the financial data reports on the 10 ratios that tell you whether your profitability is increasing, how productive your employees are, and whether you are headed for a cash flow, collections, inventory, or debt problem.
3. You receive a graph and explanation of your trends by email.

How Do You Get Started?

Send us last year's year-end profit and loss statement and balance sheet. We will review it to ensure that your financial statements are in good shape to perform a monthly financial health checkup. If they are, then you'll be asked to send us at least one and preferably two years of monthly data so we can accurately perform the trend analysis.

Garbage in Equals Garbage Out

If your financial statements are not accurate enough to perform a monthly financial health checkup, we will suggest where to go to get help cleaning up your financial statements so they can be analyzed accurately.

For more information go to www.businessfinancialhealthcheckup. com.

ACKNOWLEDGMENTS

This book would never have been written without you, my clients, over the past 40+ years.

Thank you for allowing me to help you grow profitably and build wealth. As one of you said, I have helped you grow profitably and sell your company for millions.

To Brenda Bethea, who has been my "right arm" for more than 30 years. She has participated in the growth, heard your stories, and been in the trenches with me for this entire journey.

To my parents, who guided my early years and helped shape the woman I have become. Although I didn't always appreciate your actions, you were always there to pick up the pieces when I made mistakes and cheer me on when I was working to achieve a goal.

To my late husband, Bob, who during that last conversation we had told me to "Do my thing." This book, the third I have written since he passed, is a result of our conversation.

And finally, to my daughter, Kate. Your journey is under way. I hope that you find happiness and success and build a recurring revenue program. Use the stories in this book to help you avoid mistakes and heartaches.

Thank you all. I love and appreciate you.

ABOUT THE AUTHOR

Profitability guru Ruth King is the president of Business Ventures Corporation. Ruth has a passion for helping businesses get and stay profitable.

She is especially proud of one small business owner she helped climb out of a big hole. He started with a negative $400,000 net worth 20 years ago and is still in business today...profitably and with a positive net worth.

After twelve years on the road, doing 200 flights per year, she knew there had to be a better way to reach businesspeople who wanted to build their businesses and train their employees. She began training on the internet in 1998 and began the first television-like broadcasting in 2002. Her channels include www.hvacchannel.tv and www.profitabilityrevolution.com.

Ruth holds an MBA in finance from Georgia State University and bachelor's and master's degrees in chemical engineering from Tufts University and the University of Pennsylvania, respectively.

She started the Decatur, Georgia, branch of the Small Business Development Center in 1982. She also started the Women's Entrepreneurial Center and taught a year-long course for women who wanted to start their own businesses. This course was the foundation for one of the classes at the Women's Economic Development Authority in Atlanta, Georgia.

Ruth was the instructor for the Inner City Entrepreneur program in conjunction with the Small Business Administration. This 16-week course taught business owners with at least $400,000 in revenues (and many had over $1,000,000 in revenues) how to grow to the next level. A large part of the curriculum was aimed at improving the financial knowledge of the business owners enrolled in the course.

Ruth is passionate about helping adults learn to read, photography, and marathon races (she has run 14, including two Boston Marathons).

She helped start an adult literacy organization in 1986 that currently serves over 1,000 adults per year.

Her number one 1 bestselling book, *The Courage to Be Profitable*, was named as one of the 37 books all startup businesses should read by London-based Fupping. She joins esteemed authors Napoleon Hill, Dale Carnegie, Stephen Covey, Richard Branson, and others on this list. *The Courage to Be Profitable* explains how to get and stay profitable in less than 30 minutes a month—in English rather than accounting babble. She is also the author of four other award-winning books: *Profit or Wealth?*, *The Ugly Truth about Cash*, *The Ugly Truth about Small Business*, and *The Ugly Truth about Managing People*.

Go to www.ruthking.info or email rking@ontheribbon.com to contact Ruth.

A free ebook edition is available with the purchase of this book.

To claim your free ebook edition:

1. Visit MorganJamesBOGO.com
2. Sign your name CLEARLY in the space
3. Complete the form and submit a photo of the entire copyright page
4. You or your friend can download the ebook to your preferred device

Morgan James
BOGO™

A **FREE** ebook edition is available for you or a friend with the purchase of this print book.

CLEARLY SIGN YOUR NAME ABOVE

Instructions to claim your free ebook edition:
1. Visit MorganJamesBOGO.com
2. Sign your name CLEARLY in the space above
3. Complete the form and submit a photo of this entire page
4. You or your friend can download the ebook to your preferred device

Print & Digital Together Forever.

Snap a photo

Free ebook

Read anywhere